Morning and Evening

A Parish Celebration

Joyce Ann Zimmerman, CPPS

 LITURGY TRAINING PUBLICATIONS

Acknowledgments

Editor: Kathy Luty
Production editor: Deborah Bogaert
Designer: Anna Manhart
Typesetting: Mark Hollopeter

About the cover and interior art:
This photo shows geometric, decorative carvings popular during the iconoclastic era, and the rough textures (partly due to erosion) of an arch in a Christian church in the valley of Göreme in the region of Cappadocia (presently central Turkey). Hundreds of small underground gathering places like this, well suited to recluses, were carved out of the soft tufa (volcanic rock) in the rock faces and cliffs of this region. The original photo was taken by Andy Manhart and then colorized by the designer for the cover.

This book was set in Giovanni and Gill Sans and printed by Bawden Printing Inc. of Eldridge, Iowa.

Zimmerman, Joyce Ann, 1945 –
   Morning and evening: a parish celebration/Joyce Ann Zimmerman.
      p. cm.
   Includes bibliographical references.
   ISBN 1-56854-117-1
   1.Catholic Church. Liturgy of the hours (U.S., et al.)
2. Divine office. 3. Catholic Church — United States — Liturgy — History and criticism. I. Title.
BX2000.Z56   1996
264'.0201 — dc20   96-33858
                                                         CIP

Contents

Introduction

It was a long time ago, but I remember it as if it were yesterday: my first day in the convent. It was unlike any other day I had known. The simple, chanted prayers drew me inexorably into the mystery, awe and majesty of the God who was the center of my life. Frequently throughout the day — in the morning, at midday, in the late afternoon and again in the evening — we gathered to sing God's praise and give thanks for our abundant blessings.

I never grew tired of the quiet and persistent call to daily prayer in community. The coming together at regular intervals throughout the day nurtured and sustained me. It was a source of strength — whether I was tired or discouraged, energetic or playful, searching or peaceful — to pray with others at these key hours of the day. It gave me a strong sense of being part of something much larger than myself.

Despite its recent history as the prayer of priests and religious, the Liturgy of the Hours, especially morning and evening prayer, is the daily prayer of the whole church. All who have been baptized into Christ are called to join their voices in this prayer of praise. Daily we are privileged to celebrate the mystery of Christ and his wonderful deeds of salvation on our behalf. Central to the celebration of the Liturgy of the Hours, with its rhythm of prayer at regular intervals throughout the day, are the primary (or "hinge") hours of morning and evening prayer.

Morning and evening prayer might involve a large assembly, several ministers, choir and instrumentalists, processions and incense. Or, morning and evening prayer might be prayed by the members of a household or parish committee, who would follow a very simple structure with quiet recitation and pauses for reflection. Common to both celebrations, however, is a spirit of praise and petition based on psalms and intercessions that are thematically tied to the particular time of day. The psalms and intercessory prayer form the backbone of this liturgy.

Regular participation in the Liturgy of the Hours frames our days with prayer. In the morning we give thanks for the gift of a new day and place both its joys and sorrows in God's strong hands. In the evening we express our gratitude for the blessings of the day and offer prayers for the needs of all people. At both sunrise and sunset, we gather to remember God's faithful presence and to recall our ultimate home with the Lord.

Morning and Evening: A Parish Celebration aspires to promote the celebration of the Liturgy of the Hours on the parish level. The long and varied history of this prayer attests to its power.

Whenever we begin something new, the temptation is just to plunge in and try it. A more gradual approach, however, is suggested in this book. The first three chapters set the foundation. Chapter one examines the rhythm of everyday living and its relationship to daily prayer. Chapter two traces the development of the Liturgy of the Hours, from the church's early years to the present day. The 1971 revision of the rite is explored in chapter three.

The final two chapters focus more directly on suggestions for implementation: Chapter four takes a closer look at the structure and flow of morning and evening prayer, and chapter five is filled with practical ideas for celebrating the Liturgy of the Hours in the parish or in other settings, such as on a college campus or in a hospital or religious community. Successful implementation depends on a thorough understanding of the theology and structure of the Liturgy of the Hours. *This is the key to sustained success.*

The Liturgy of the Hours is not a *choice* for parishes or other Christian communities, nor is it a luxury embraced by "professionals" who seem to have more time to devote to such esoteric prayer practices. It is clear from the church's early tradition that *the Liturgy of the Hours is the usual daily prayer of the church.* Period. No qualifications. It is not a substitute prayer that a parish may schedule when a priest is unavailable for daily Mass, nor is it an "occasional prayer" to be scheduled only during special seasons or on feast days. *The Liturgy of the Hours is the usual daily prayer of the church.*

We Christians frequently assemble for liturgical prayer. That coming together, be it weekly or daily, is central to the life of any Christian. Surrounded by pleasures which do not satisfy, we acknowledge a deep hunger for encounter with the God who alone suffices. Liturgical prayer opens the door to that possibility. The daily gathering of believers provides us with a glimpse of that heavenly liturgy where one day we will forever enjoy the lavishness of the heavenly banquet. Together we sing — shout — a joyful song unto our God who calls us to such riches.

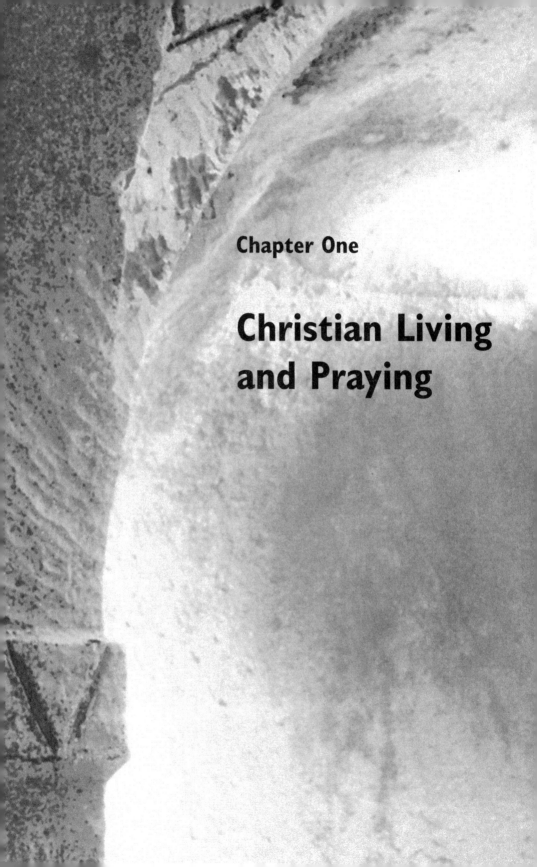

Chapter One

Christian Living
and Praying

How odd it is that life's most significant moments sometimes find us totally oblivious to their import: A casual meeting with a stranger turns out to be our first glimpse of a future spouse; or an ordinary visit with a dear friend becomes the last time we ever see her. Similarly, our entrance into the Christian community is often unremarkable. Most of us, baptized as infants, have no recollection of the event. But like all sacraments, baptism reaches beyond its ritual celebration into the very fabric of our living and being. Those of us baptized as adults likely have more vivid recollections of baptism's transforming powers, especially now that more and more parishes are placing renewed emphasis on the actions of being plunged into and washed by living waters.

Saint Paul, in his letter to the Romans, writes:

> Do you not know that all of us who have been baptized
> into Christ Jesus were baptized into his death? Therefore
> we have been buried with him by baptism into death,
> so that, just as Christ was raised from the dead by the glory
> of the Father, so we too might walk in newness of life.
> (Romans 6: 3 – 4)

This image of dying and rising is key to understanding baptism. A well-celebrated rite of baptism draws us into this rhythm of new life through death — the one to be baptized is plunged into the baptismal waters (a symbolic dying to the old self) and then led out of the waters and clothed in a white garment (a symbolic rising to new life). This ritual action vividly proclaims the profound transformation that is taking place. Through baptism we become members of the body of Christ and are called to live as Christ lived.

Liturgical Prayer

That is precisely what our liturgy is all about. It is the assembly of baptized Christians, a visible body united to Christ its head, who gather to celebrate the sacred mysteries of Jesus' life, death and resurrection. It is misleading, though, to think of the paschal mystery as referring only to Jesus and to events limited to a particular historical time and geographic locale. In that context we gain the benefits of Jesus' actions on our behalf, but we are not involved in the unfolding mystery itself. In limiting the meaning to the historical events, we shortchange both the paschal mystery and our own involvement in that mystery. In reality, the significance of those events reaches far beyond the events themselves. Liturgy is our privileged means for making present the death and resurrection of Jesus here and now.

The inherent power of the liturgy, however, lies not in what we do in the liturgy but in what the liturgy does to us. Liturgy transforms. It transforms us ever more perfectly into the body of Christ, and herein lies the connection between Christian living and prayer: The transformation that is proper to liturgy directly affects all that we are and all that we do. Our liturgical rituals challenge us to live the paschal mystery, to open our lives to that rhythm of dying to self and rising in Christ. It is impossible to grasp the depth of that mystery in a single celebration, liturgical season or cycle. The transformation we long for is accomplished gradually, through the daily, weekly and yearly rhythm of celebrations that draw us ever deeper into the Mystery of all mysteries. Time, as Robert Tuzik pointed out in *Christ Living Among His People* (Washington, DC: Federation of Diocesan Liturgical Commissions, 1984), becomes our entry point into the paschal mystery.

Rhythm of Living and Praying

As human beings, we are bonded to one another through our common experience of time. Shared memories of the first moon landing, the assassination of President Kennedy or the explosion of the Space Shuttle Challenger bridge the gulf that often divides us. Time is both intensely personal and profoundly universal. We name our experience of time in many ways. On the cultural level we identify calendar years, fiscal years, academic years and election years. We know daylight saving time, tax time, even Miller time! On a personal level, engaged couples, counting the days until their wedding, experience time differently than does a person with a terminal illness. Our calendars reveal much about our identity.

The church, too, names its experience of time in unique ways. Advent/Christmas, Lent/Easter, holy days and fast days reveal to us possibilities for recognizing the paschal mystery and its transforming power in our lives. Our liturgical celebrations unfold within our human experience of time. Daily, weekly and yearly, we shape and are shaped by these natural cycles.

Daily cycle

Our days are measured by a regular pattern of waking and sleeping, even at a time in history when our actions and activities are no longer directly controlled by the sun's rising and setting. Electric lights have allowed us to turn night into day, yet we are often more closely tied to the sun's rising and setting than we sometimes recognize. All living creatures are affected by and respond to the earth's movement around the sun. Is not daylight saving time an attempt to adjust light to the rhythm of our contemporary lives?

Similarly, this daily rhythm of light and darkness has significance for our Christian living and praying. Each day reflects the ancient rhythm of dying and rising. Evening and morning have long been instinctive times for people to turn toward God. It comes as no surprise then that sunrise and sunset are favored times for prayer. They are natural times to pause and reflect on who we are and how we are to live. We begin and end each day by placing our cares and our joys in the loving hands of God. But as significant as each day is, we are aware of yet another, broader rhythm in our lives. Day follows day and day follows day, until soon a weekly pattern emerges from the steady march of time.

Weekly cycle

Not all the days of the week are the same. Blue Mondays, midweek slumps and long weekends vary the rhythm of our lives. Liturgically, too, our prayer is shaped by this weekly cycle. Fasting and feasting color our days. From the very beginning, Christians would meet regularly on Sunday, the first day of the week, for the breaking of the bread. Eucharist is a celebration of the risen Lord's presence, and so Sunday, the day of resurrection, is the naturally symbolic day for its celebration. Sunday is the church's first and oldest feast day.

The weekly rhythm is also shaped by the way Christians keep Fridays. Friday has customarily been a day of fasting and penance in the church. Until the renewal of Vatican II, Roman Catholics abstained from meat on Fridays, the day the Lord suffered and died. Although this particular law is no longer in effect, we are still called to fast and do penance on Fridays. Thus a weekly pattern of dying and rising, of fasting and feasting, emerges from our days.

Yearly cycle

The daily celebration of dying and rising culminating in the weekly celebration of resurrection has yet a third expression in the liturgical year. In the course of a year, the birth, life, death, resurrection and ascension of the Lord, as well as the coming of the Spirit at Pentecost, become the prism through which we see reflected our own participation in the mystery of salvation. Advent/Christmas, Lent/Easter, Pentecost and Ordinary Time flesh out for us the promise of our redemption.

These three rhythms — daily, weekly, yearly — flow into one another. Our Christian religious experience is holistic, unfolding gradually throughout each of the segments of time in which we live. For most of us, however, our formal prayer has been limited to weekly and yearly occasions. We are invited now to recover a pattern of daily liturgical prayer. This recovery opens up for us the fullness of the church's treasury of prayer.

Recovery of the Liturgy of the Hours

Our desire to recover the Liturgy of the Hours as the usual daily prayer of the church stems from what is so familiar to us: the rising and setting of the sun, the promise and fulfillment each day holds for us. The rhythm of our daily life is the driving force for the rhythm of our liturgical life. This is why the recovery of the Liturgy of the Hours as the usual daily prayer for the whole church is so promising and so exciting. It is a critical link fortifying the connection between what we profess and what we live.

Desire of the church

The Liturgy of the Hours, unfamiliar to many Catholics, has long been understood to be the privileged prayer of priests and those members of religious orders bound by their constitutions to pray it. Even the nineteen paragraphs in the *Constitution on the Sacred Liturgy* devoted to the Liturgy of the Hours imply that this prayer is largely the domain of clerics and religious, although several paragraphs clearly indicate that it is the whole church joined to Christ that continues the tradition of pausing regularly at key times of the day to offer a canticle of divine praise.

This acknowledgment is most clear in the *Constitution on the Sacred Liturgy,* #100, which explicitly asks pastors to celebrate morning and especially evening prayer with the people on Sundays and on special feasts. This paragraph ends by encouraging the laity — together with the priests, among themselves or even individually — to pray the Liturgy of the Hours. Thus the *Constitution on the Sacred Liturgy* took the first steps toward recovering the ancient tradition of the Hours as the people's daily prayer. Twenty-some years later, however, we are not much further along the road.

Why <u>Parish</u> Liturgy of the Hours?

First of all, by reason of their baptism, the rhythm of dying and rising defines all Christians. At baptism we are plunged into the waters of death so that we might rise anew to live as members of the body of Christ. The Liturgy of the Hours, as the daily expression of this rhythm, belongs to all Christians. Living and praying this rhythm is not the privilege of a select few. Rather, it is the heartbeat of the whole body of Christ.

Furthermore, the church as the people of God — as the body of Christ — is a *community*. Just as God is a trinity of persons, so the church is a plurality of persons. Just as each person of the Trinity is inextricably related to the other divine persons, so each member of the body

7

is inextricably bound up with others in the same shared identity. This suggests that the normative liturgical prayer is communal. Personal, private prayer is necessary and leads us to liturgical prayer. But it is in coming together as a liturgical assembly before our God that the church is most visible. Liturgical prayer, then, is necessarily a communal act of a people united as one body in charity and love. The liturgical assembly is a manifestation of church. It is the primary witness we give to who we are — the body of Christ. And this witness is, ideally, a daily one.

Parish celebrations of the Liturgy of the Hours are also desirable because it is there that we are baptized and celebrate the eucharist. Celebrating morning and evening prayer in the parish helps us connect that prayer with our baptismal identity and with the weekly celebration of the eucharist. It makes the daily, weekly and yearly rhythms of the paschal mystery visible in the same sacred space. Faithfulness to this prayer reminds us that Christianity cannot be a once-a-week religious experience. We surrender ourselves daily to the transforming power of communal ritual.

Parish Liturgy of the Hours also helps us keep a sharp distinction between our own devotional prayers and liturgical prayer, which is the prayer of the whole church. Although it is certainly possible to pray the Liturgy of the Hours alone — even desirable if the alternative is not to pray it at all — the preferred option is to pray with the local church, the body visibly gathered. There is a kind of "dying" to actually leaving our comfortable homes or apartments in order to gather elsewhere with others to pray liturgically. Realistically our daily schedules and demands would hardly permit each of us to be present in our parish each morning and evening, yet assembling at least occasionally for daily prayer both prepares us for a more fruitful celebration of the eucharist and sustains in us its benefits.

One very practical reason for celebrating the Liturgy of the Hours in the parish is that most of us develop and sustain good habits when we have concrete structures in place that promote them. We are more likely to pray morning and evening prayer if we have a parish community to support us. When our enthusiasm wanes, we are sustained by the faith of others. We, in turn, can support and sustain them when necessary.

Ultimately the Liturgy of the Hours bridges the gap between our daily living and our religious experience. In the simple rhythm of morning and evening, we discover the deepest meaning of our Christian living. Prayer is no longer "time out" of the ordinary; it becomes a sancti-fication of the ordinary. Gradually the ordinary reveals to us its deeper dimensions; all of life is redeemed and brought back to God's loving embrace. Together, each morning and evening, we join our voices in a prayer of praise and thanksgiving.

Chapter Two

Lessons from History

The simple but bold bid to "pray without ceasing" (1 Thessalonians 5:17) has grounded the pattern of Christian prayer from the very beginning. Jesus surely showed us the way. The gospels (especially the Gospel of Luke) frequently mention that Jesus prayed in the synagogue and in the temple. At other times he withdrew to a quiet place. Prayer — basking in God's presence — is an instinctive response to a God who loves intimately and unfailingly.

Although Christian literature abounds with references to prayer, it is no small task to reconstruct with accuracy the prayer life of early Christians. It is equally difficult to trace the development of their prayer to the patterns we practice in the church today. The Liturgy of the Hours is one of those prayer patterns. A brief survey of the development of the Liturgy of the Hours can help us reflect on the basic structures and content of that prayer; it will also provide a solid foundation for the pastoral judgments we need to make as we seek to implement the Liturgy of the Hours on the parish level.

History, we realize, can prove elusive. The recovery of "what was" is less precise than we sometimes imagine; the temptation is to read back into history our own perceptions or convictions. Given these cautions, in this chapter we trace the main lines of the inception and development of the Liturgy of the Hours. We divide our brief chronicle into five broad, sometimes overlapping, periods. Our goal is simply to summarize the data and draw conclusions that shed some light on the development of the church's daily prayer.

Early Christian Prayer Patterns

The first three centuries of Christian history provide scant evidence for reconstructing any kind of set prayer times, structures or content. There is no doubt, though, that early Christians prayed. They prayed unceasingly. They prayed at fixed times. They favored prayer at the beginning and end of the day. They prayed both alone and in common. They prayed in Jesus' name.

Many New Testament passages mention prayer. Sometimes these references describe Jesus or others at prayer (Luke 9:18, 28; Acts 10:9), and sometimes they are an exhortation or a command to pray (Luke 18:1 – 8 and 11:9 – 10). A few passages instruct us on how to pray (Luke 11:2 – 4), and there are a few examples of actual prayers and hymns (Luke 22: 42, John 17 or Philippians 2:6 – 11, for example). The Acts of the Apostles alone contains no fewer than twenty-six references to prayer.

No example of a complete daily prayer exists from the first three centuries of the Christian era, so it is difficult to reconstruct a model with accuracy. Although liturgical historians disagree about the extent to which early Christian prayer is related to or dependent on Jewish prayer practices, it can hardly be disputed that the pattern of daily prayer familiar to Jews — both in frequency and in content — would have influenced the way Christians prayed. Both the times for prayer (morning, afternoon, evening and night) and the character of that prayer (primarily praise and blessing) are common to both Jewish and early Christian prayer.

The *Didache (The Teaching of the Twelve Apostles)* is an early Christian document roughly contemporary with the New Testament writings. It gives us the first concrete evidence of a directive on daily prayer when it exhorts Christians to pray the Lord's Prayer three times each day (*Didache* 8:3). This is an important reference because it gives early evidence of an established custom of marking the course of the day with prayer. Clement of Rome, a late-first-century author who wrote a letter to the church at Corinth, also gives us some insight into Christian prayer patterns at the turn of the century. In Clement's *First*

Letter we discover that Christians prayed with outstretched hands and at specific times of the day. His reference to sunset and sunrise as marking the death and resurrection of the Lord is the first example of Christian symbolism connected to specific times of the day. Praise was a constant theme for prayer — Clement includes ten doxologies at key places in his letter. Intercessory prayer is also mentioned.

By the third century, references to daily Christian prayer habits became more abundant. We can glean a bit more information from this period, but an elaborately structured or universal system of daily prayer had not yet been developed. Clement of Alexandria *(Stromata VII)* mentions the customs of facing east during prayer and of praying at the third, sixth and ninth hours of the day (9:00 AM, 12:00 noon and 3:00 PM, respectively). These were the three Roman divisions of the day and may have been the inspiration for Christians to pray at these particular times. Clement hastens to add, however, that Christians praise God at all times.

The third-century writer Tertullian provides a motivation for praying at these hours: the third hour recalls the coming of the Spirit at Pentecost; the sixth imitates Peter at prayer at Joppa (Acts 11:5); and the ninth hour follows the example of Peter and John going to the temple to pray (Acts 3:1). Tertullian also makes references to prayer at midnight, to the combining of psalms and readings as the format for prayer, and to the use of Christian hymns during prayer. Perhaps most important for our purposes, Tertullian notes that morning and evening prayer are obligatory.

Another third-century writer, Hippolytus, mentions instructions from the bishop (the usual presider at liturgy in the Christian communities at that time) as part of morning prayer. He also mentions prayer at midnight *(Apostolic Traditions* 31, 33, 35). It is significant that Hippolytus set Christian daily prayer in the framework of the paschal mystery. Night prayer highlights the second coming of Christ, while morning prayer, with its themes of light, emphasizes the resurrection. The third hour recalls Jesus nailed to the cross, the sixth hour the beginning of great darkness, and the ninth hour the piercing and death of Jesus. By the end of the third century, then, the evidence indicates that daily prayer was both private and communal, frequent (up to six times during the day) and beginning to develop a thematic rationale. In all of this, however, the original inspiration to "pray without ceasing" remained paramount.

"Cathedral" Response

The church developed more elaborate forms of daily prayer after Constantine's early-fourth-century "Edict of Milan," which effectively ended persecutions and granted Christians the freedom to practice their religion publicly. We have numerous examples of daily prayer from this period, characterized by a rich variety because the centralization of the Western church had not yet occurred. Local churches remained relatively autonomous.

One pattern of prayer developed in fourth-century cathedrals, the equivalent of today's parish — hence the name "cathedral" style of praying. This cathedral style was especially dominant in Eastern church communities, where a richness of style prevailed. Evidence suggests that daily prayer was a public ritual geared toward a communal gathering. The psalms and prayers formed its backbone. It was highly structured, generally invariable and full of color, movement and music. The psalms were sung responsorially: a cantor would introduce a short, melodic response and the assembly would repeat it. Then the cantor would sing the psalm, which the assembly would affirm by their common response. The intercessory prayer was chanted as a litany, the length of which depended on the occasion and the community. Communal prayer was celebrated at the two natural times of morning and evening; each time had its own spirit.

Morning prayer began at sunrise and celebrated the resurrection: as the sun rose, so did the Son. Christians also praised God for the blessing of a new day. The general pattern shows that morning prayer included Psalm 63 (the invariable morning psalm), Psalms 148 – 150 (the great praise psalms), collect prayers, the Gloria (in the Eastern churches), invocations (a litany of praise and intercessions addressed to the risen Christ) and a blessing and dismissal.

Evening prayer was scheduled at sundown and served as a transition between the end of one day and the beginning of the next. Its general pattern included three main parts. It began with a light service, or *lucernarium*, which included a proclamation and thanksgiving for Christ the Light, an evening hymn and an opening collect. This focus on light in the gathering darkness reminded Christians that Christ the Light had come into the world to dispel darkness. The second part consisted of responsorial psalmody, especially Psalm 141, and one or more evening psalms that often emphasized the theme of thanksgiving. The Canticle of Mary *(Magnificat)* followed. Intercessions formed the third part of the prayer. They were general prayers for the whole church and for the world; the last petition was always for those who had died that day. Evening prayer, like morning praise, concluded with a blessing and dismissal.

Each local community was relatively free to develop its own style of daily prayer, and so we have a good number of extant prayers to study. Granting minor differences, certain similarities in structure and style become apparent. The cathedral tradition was primarily a prayer of praise and thanksgiving. It was not a word service. In fact in most cases, proclamation of the word and preaching were not regular features of morning and evening prayer.

Who prayed?

Naturally, it would have been virtually impossible for everyone to be present every day for morning and evening prayer. But their common identity as the body of Christ enabled the whole community to "pray without ceasing" even when other responsibilities kept them from communal prayer. The body was united with the head in one unceasing chorus of praise.

Some Christians withdrew from mainstream Christianity in order to literally "pray without ceasing." Thus alongside the cathedral style of prayer, there emerged a parallel "monastic" practice of daily prayer. This monastic pattern flourished particularly in the Western church.

"Monastic" Response

Monastics had the luxury of built-in time to pray, which few outside the monastery could enjoy. Consequently, the monastics introduced several additional periods of prayer during the day. A full monastic Office would eventually include Matins (very early morning prayer, reminiscent of the night prayer of the earlier period), Lauds (morning prayer at sunrise), Prime (first hour, about 6:00 AM), Terce (third hour, 9:00 AM), Sext (sixth hour, noon), None (ninth hour, 3:00 PM), Vespers (sundown) and Compline (prayer just before retiring at night). Because the short, invariable, ceremonial style of the cathedrals was barely suited to such extended prayer, the monastic communities developed their own "monastic" style.

Monastic principles

Two new principles guided the development of prayer in the monasteries of the West. First, the entire psalter was prayed during a given period of time, usually one week. Obviously, this meant that a greater number of psalms were used during each period of prayer. The cathedral ideal of selecting certain psalms appropriate to either morning or evening was abandoned in favor of a pattern of assigning psalms to the various Hours in numerical sequence to cover all 150 psalms in the given period of time. Furthermore, the responsorial style that was so appropriate to the community gathered around the bishop in the cathedral gave way to a recited style, prayed aloud by a single monk (or sometimes several taking turns). The psalms then became the basis for reflection and meditation. Rather than functioning as expressions of praise and celebration, they became avenues for sustaining the contemplative prayer of the monastic community.

A second principle operative in the development of the monastic office was that of *lectio continua,* the sequential reading of scripture designed to cover the entire Bible in the course of a year. Unlike the cathedral office, the monastic office invariably included a reading of the word. The pure prayer of praise that characterized the cathedral style of worship gradually became longer and more frequent to satisfy the reflective needs of the monastics. Extended periods of private prayer between the psalms were conducive to contemplation, while the scripture lessons provided edification. Basic to the monastic style then was quiet contemplation of the divine mysteries sustained throughout the entire day.

Differences in Development

The earliest strata of Eastern monasticism shows the monastics praying at morning and evening, as did the cathedral communities. However, because the monastic ideal was to pray always, the structure of their prayer reflected this goal. Basically, early monastic prayer was a flexible combination of scripture and prayer that fit their contemplative needs.

Thus, different approaches to the Liturgy of the Hours took root. In the West, monasticism took the lead in developing the more complicated daily prayer structure outlined earlier. Its basic shape consisted of psalmody, scripture readings and intercessions. Benedict added a hymn to conclude the psalmody.

Mingling: "Urban" Offices

Eventually some monasteries became attached to the great cathedral centers, and an era of "urban monasticism" arose. It is no surprise that this brought about a mixture of the cathedral and monastic styles. As the Office gained in complexity, other elements (such as litanies) were added, making it lengthier and musically complex. Skilled professionals, or "canons," whose primary ministry was to sing the Office, were needed at the cathedrals to celebrate daily prayer. These "canons" then became the regular choir that assured the full celebration of the Hours. Often they were joined by others; sometimes the laity were present.

Until about the thirteenth century, there was still great diversity in the Liturgy of the Hours in both Eastern and Western churches. Even after the monastics came into contact with the cathedrals, causing an inevitable mix of the two styles of prayer, the Hours still remained a communal prayer with no sense of individual obligation to pray the Office. Eventually, however, other circumstances challenged its communal and popular celebration.

Breviaries: Private Clerical Prayer

During the medieval period many of the parochial clergy were bound up in the alliances between civil and ecclesial authority that were so typical of the feudal church. Often they were anything but concerned with the spiritual well-being of their parishioners. The founding of the great mendicant orders (Franciscans and Dominicans) provided the laity with caring shepherds. These itinerant preachers were a breath of fresh air in a stale, tightly controlled and often corrupt church-society.

Ironically enough, what proved to be a positive development for the spiritual growth of the medieval laity proved to be a detriment to the communal celebration of the Liturgy of the Hours. Singing the complex and lengthy choral Offices was impossible for the simple brothers who traveled the highways and byways ministering to the common people. Shorter manuscripts ("breviaries," from the Latin word meaning "short") provided a compromise solution to this very practical problem. These new manuscripts were more portable and could easily be taken along on the mendicants' journeys.

Because these itinerant preachers traveled widely, their style of prayer quickly spread over a very large part of Western Christendom. To some extent, this brought about a standardization of the Liturgy of the Hours, although there was still much adaptation to local custom.

Breakdown

A combination of factors contributed to the breakdown of the Liturgy of the Hours as the daily communal prayer of the whole body of Christ: Clergy who were inadequately formed for their sacred duties, corrupt clergy who had no desire to pray and itinerant clergy who prayed simple Offices all contributed to a drastic change in the nature and purpose of the Liturgy of the Hours. By the time of the Reformation in 1517, the Liturgy of the Hours was well on its way to becoming an obligatory prayer recited privately by the clergy.

The Council of Trent (1545 – 1563), as it did in so many other areas of church life, called for a reform of the Divine Office (as the Liturgy of the Hours was then known). The 1568 *Breviary of Pius V* was primarily monastic in style. It contained both a great number of sequential psalms distributed over a single week and longer readings from scripture and from patristic sources. Yet the inclusion of antiphons, for example, suggests that its choral character stubbornly survived. Those in major orders were required by church law to recite the breviary daily, which solidly established the Liturgy of the Hours as a private prayer. Many priests lived alone or had an understanding of communal living and praying which differs significantly from our own.

In the wake of the Council of Trent, the Divine Office became almost exclusively the domain of clerics and monastics whose rule required them to pray it in choir. Nevertheless, its character as the daily prayer of the church was retained in some regions. Even into this century, German immigrant parishes in North America prayed Sunday Vespers with the laity in attendance. It should be noted, however, that although the laity were present, they essentially took part only by listening or by praying their own private devotions (as they did at Mass). The daily communal prayer of the church had become, for all practical purposes, the private, devotional prayer of the clergy and monastics.

Lessons from History

What does all of this mean for us? It is usually a mistake to think that we can simply return to an earlier era and uncritically implement its practices. So we are faced with the question, "What is normative?" It is also clear that the church and modern society have changed significantly since the fourth to sixth centuries, when liturgical practices developed prolifically. Although we learn from history, we must nevertheless interpret its lessons for our own times and needs. These brief reflections on the development of the Liturgy of the Hours open up several key issues.

Creativity and adaptation

The Liturgy of the Hours is the daily prayer of the whole church in which each one of us participates by reason of our baptism. Gathering to celebrate the Liturgy of the Hours is the usual daily manifestation of the presence of the risen body of Christ. A liturgical assembly gathered to celebrate the Liturgy of the Hours is, at the same time, a manifestation of the church. It is a revelation of the Christian community, because the paschal mystery defines our very identity.

Though the Liturgy of the Hours defines and crystallizes our identity as a Christian community, its history also warns us to be open to adaptations suited to different times and circumstances. The *Constitution on the Sacred Liturgy* (#50) was sensitive to this historical lesson in its call to simplify the rites, to eliminate duplicate elements or disadvantageous historical accretions and to restore those elements that had been lost. Just as the invariability of cathedral style is hardly suited to the numerous prayer periods and reflective needs of monastics, the length and frequency of monastic prayer is not well-suited to the normal routines of parish and family life.

The eventual blend of cathedral and monastic styles offers us some leeway in our choices. Today we are faced not only with the task of implementing the Liturgy of the Hours in our liturgical communities but also with discovering, probably by trial and error, the unique combination of structural elements and styles that suits our time and our prayer needs. The Liturgy of the Hours requires creativity and adaptation if it is to be restored as the usual, daily prayer of the People of God.

Full expression

Daily, weekly and yearly, the community of believers gathers to give praise and thanks for the dying and rising in the life of Jesus and in our own lives as well. The paschal mystery is so rich that only with full implementation of the church's liturgical rituals do we come to a broader vision of Christ's redeeming sacrifice. We ought to think twice before we neglect any of these rich expressions of the paschal mystery.

Finally, but no less significantly, our historical reflections advocate liturgical prayer as a *way of life* for Christians. *Liturgical spirituality* is the basic expression of Christian living. For anyone who professes to be Christian, the Liturgy of the Hours is the usual, daily liturgical expression of that commitment.

Making history work for us

This brief sketch of the development of the Liturgy of the Hours shows us the unique relationship between practice and understanding. As the practice of the Liturgy of the Hours changed — because of complex social and political conditions in both the church and society — so did the church's understanding of it. Only with knowledge of these factors and the way they have contributed to our concrete religious practice can we begin to implement the Liturgy of the Hours with some hope of success.

Those who are responsible for choosing a particular form of prayer for their liturgical community may need to consider some basic questions: What were the ecclesial and societal factors that led to the acceptance of the "cathedral" style of the Liturgy of the Hours as the daily prayer of the church? Are there any parallels in our contemporary situation? What elements of monasticism contributed to the development of an alternative style of daily prayer for monastics? Do any of those factors apply to us today? What elements of cathedral style were unsuitable for monastics? What elements of monastic style were unsuitable for cathedral prayer? What new ecclesial and societal factors affect parochial prayer today? What mix of elements might be used? What new stylistic elements may be needed?

The challenge of the *Constitution on the Sacred Liturgy* to revise the church's liturgical rites certainly applied to the Liturgy of the Hours; the revised rite of the Liturgy of the Hours was promulgated in 1971. But its revision failed to escape the inherent tension between cathedral and monastic styles. We turn now to an analysis of that rite.

Chapter Three

The 1971 Revision of the Liturgy of the Hours

I f there were a simple and foolproof solution to the problem of liturgical renewal, someone surely would have come up with it by now. But obviously, there is no such solution. We continue to plod along, and the challenge of renewal is further tested by widely differing approaches to liturgical practices which often lead to confusion and entrenchment.

It is always difficult to balance the tension between the need for rubrics and regulations and the desire to be faithful to the tradition and its requirements for continued renewal. The original revision of the church's Latin rite for the Liturgy of the Hours was completed less than a decade after the promulgation of the *Constitution on the Sacred Liturgy* in 1963. It is not surprising that now, after several decades of practice, we find ourselves examining the strengths and weaknesses of those revisions. The revised rites brought about a great deal of necessary *adaptation*, but the real work of *renewal* is just beginning. Moreover, that renewal will never be completed. We must constantly adapt and continually revive our renewal efforts.

The average North American parish or liturgical community is still struggling to adopt the vision of liturgy called for by the Council. When the yearning for good liturgical celebrations is overshadowed by apathy, the local liturgy committee often scrambles for new approaches to rouse the assembly to fervor. That is a natural and perhaps necessary rehearsal — paving the way for real renewal. Now, however, the time is ripe for the work of renewal to flower. A close look at the revised rite of the Liturgy of the Hours gives us a sense of both the broad vision and the technical details that were part of the first stage of renewal.

Promulgation

The revision and implementation of a liturgical rite is a complex process. Pope Paul VI promulgated the revised rite for the Liturgy of the Hours when he issued the Apostolic Constitution *Laudis canticum* on November 1, 1970. His hopes for the revision were eloquently summed up:

> Now that the prayer of the holy Church has been reformed and entirely revised in keeping with its very ancient tradition and in the light of the needs of our day, it is to be hoped above all that the Liturgy of the Hours may pervade and penetrate the whole of Christian prayer, giving it life, direction, and expression and effectively nourishing the spiritual life of the people of God (#8).

Later in this same paragraph, Paul VI made explicit the realization that this prayer belongs to the whole Church:

> Everyone shares in this prayer, which is proper to the one Body as it offers prayers that give expression to the voice of Christ's beloved Bride.

The official edition of a rite is accompanied by an introduction that helps clarify the rite's intent, theology, structure and celebration. The *General Instruction of the Liturgy of the Hours* was issued on February 2, 1971. This document was issued before the actual revision of the rite was completed in order to prepare people for the changes in the rite and to facilitate its implementation. The decree *Horarum liturgia* promulgated the original Latin edition *(editio typica)* of the revised rite on April 11, 1971. The official English translation was completed in 1974.

The *General Instruction of the Liturgy of the Hours* outlines the basic structure of the Liturgy of the Hours and the way in which the various elements fit together to form an integrated prayer. It provides guidelines and options for adaptation and thus is a valuable tool for successfully implementing the Liturgy of the Hours in a parish or liturgical community. A good grasp of the principles and implications of the *General Instruction* gives us confidence that celebrating the Liturgy of the Hours on a regular basis is not as difficult as it may at first seem. Familiarity with this document assures us that the adaptations we might make are legitimate and within the parameters of the official rite.

It is beyond the scope of this work to do a detailed commentary on the *General Instruction*. This chapter will, however, briefly discuss selected points related to morning and evening prayer that make implementating the Liturgy of the Hours well within the reach of any parish or liturgical community. This commentary is the backdrop for the principles and guidelines which form the basis of our subsequent suggestions for implementation; it lays the foundation for adaptations that will enable us to implement morning and evening prayer in a parish setting. We take a positive approach to liturgical law: It is a guideline that helps us shape liturgical prayer for our particular community, and at the same time it ensures that we remain within the essential structure that makes this prayer a prayer of the whole church.

Chapter one

This first chapter of the *General Instruction*, "Importance of the Liturgy of the Hours or Divine Office in the Life of the Church," sets forth the basic scriptural and theological principles for praying the Liturgy of the Hours. Stressing that it is the prayer of Christ in the church (#3 – 7) which continues through the action of the Holy Spirit (#8), the purpose of this prayer is "to sanctify the day and the whole range of human activity" (#10 – 11). Furthermore, it extends throughout the entire day the spirit of praise and thanksgiving that is central to the eucharist (#12). The *General Instruction* makes it clear that the Liturgy of the Hours is primarily a communal prayer (#9,

#20 – 32) through which we exercise our participation in the priesthood of Christ (#13 – 14). Praise and intercession are its primary characteristics (#15 – 17).

Three points are important here. First, chapter one of the *General Instruction* emphasizes that the Liturgy of the Hours is the prayer of Christ with his church. Liturgical prayer is always ecclesial prayer, and it must be respected as such. This suggests that our adaptations need to be within the scope of the official prayer. Personal preferences and "gimmicky" options are to be avoided; we are praying the prayer of the church, not our own private prayer. Second, the Liturgy of the Hours is a communal prayer. We gather as a liturgical assembly of "two or more" in Jesus' name. Third, the Liturgy of the Hours is primarily a prayer of praise and intercession. The psalmody and intercessions must be structurally central; there are no substitutes for these two elements of the prayer.

Chapter two

Chapter two, "Sanctification of the Day: The Different Liturgical Hours," provides a brief introduction to the whole office and then comments on each specific Hour. Because our concern in this book is chiefly with morning and evening prayer, we will comment on these two Hours only.

The *General Instruction* reiterates what the *Constitution on the Sacred Liturgy* says about morning and evening prayer: They are "the two hinges on which the daily office turns" and therefore are to be regarded with the highest importance (#37, 40). Morning prayer is intended to sanctify the early hours of the day; it recalls the resurrection for us (#38). Evening prayer offers thanks for the day now spent, recalls the redemption through the offering of an evening sacrifice and looks for the coming of Christ in the dawn of a new day and again at the end of time (#39).

The next thirteen paragraphs of the *General Instruction* describe the structure of morning and evening prayer. Basically, both morning and evening prayer begin with an introductory verse and hymn. Selected psalms and a canticle, three in all, are at the heart of these Hours. A reading from the scriptures, with an optional homily and responsory, follows. A gospel canticle, intercessions, the Lord's Prayer, a concluding prayer and a blessing and dismissal complete the pattern. Directives for combining the Hours with Mass or with another Hour are given in #93 – 99. This option raises a host of issues which will be dealt with in more detail later in this book.

Chapter three

Chapter three is concerned with "Different Elements in the Liturgy of the Hours." The first four sections of this chapter (#100 – 135) deal with the psalms. The psalms come to us from a long Hebrew tradition and have great power to invoke in us sentiments of devotion and praise (#100). They express the human condition (#105 – 107). Because the psalms are inherently musical compositions, all recitations (even private ones) should keep in mind this musical character (#103). Whenever we pray the psalms in the Liturgy of the Hours, we do so as the whole church (#108) and therefore need to be aware of their full meaning, especially their messianic dimension (#109). The captions, antiphons and psalm prayers are intended to underscore the christological meaning of a psalm or to draw us into the festal season or feast being commemorated (#110 – 120).

Depending on the literary style and length of the psalm, the manner in which the psalms are sung may vary. The *General Instruction* mentions unison singing, antiphonal arrangements (between two groups of singers) or a responsorial style in which the antiphon is sung between each strophe or stanza. Each psalm concludes with the *Gloria Patri* (#121 – 125). Almost the entire psalter appears over a four-week cycle. Psalms with suitable morning or evening themes are assigned to those specific Hours. Some psalms are reserved for a particular liturgical season because they highlight the character of that season. Other psalms are associated with particular days (e.g., Sunday and Friday) because of their paschal or penitential character (#126 – 130). Three entire psalms (Psalms 78, 105 and 106) as well as portions of other psalms have been omitted because of their potentially offensive nature (#131). Long psalms are divided (#132), and the four-week cycle of assigned psalms is coordinated with the liturgical year (#133 – 135).

The *General Instruction* (#136 – 139) next focuses on the canticles, which are psalm-like songs of praise and thanksgiving. Two types of canticles are used in the revised rite. The gospel canticles — the Benedictus, Magnificat and Nunc Dimittis — are sung at morning, evening and night prayer, respectively. They culminate the psalmody and, as the *General Instruction* indicates, ought to be given the same dignity as traditionally has been associated with the proclamation of the gospel. The non-gospel, or minor, canticles are taken either from the Hebrew Scriptures or from the letters of the apostles or the Book of Revelation. The New Testament canticle is prayed *after* the two psalms at evening prayer (so that the order of the two testaments remains intact), whereas the canticle from the Hebrew Scriptures is located *between* the psalms at morning prayer. Like the psalms, the canticles are essentially musical compositions and therefore should be sung or recited in a way that highlights their musical nature.

Chapter three continues with a discussion about the readings (#140 – 168). It includes directives for the responsories, which are a kind of acclamation intended to help the word of God penetrate more deeply into our hearts (#169 – 172). The short readings assigned to morning and evening prayer fit the day, the season or the feast. They were chosen from both the Hebrew and Christian scriptures, although the latter are used exclusively at evening prayer (#158). At both morning and evening prayer, a longer reading may be chosen from either the Office of Readings or the *Lectionary for Mass* (#46).

Hymns (#173 – 178) have long been an important part of the Liturgy of the Hours. They have been retained in the revised rite. However, their structural place in the Office has changed. In both morning and evening prayer, the hymn now precedes the psalmody, which changes its function in the liturgy. Hymns are to be chosen in accord with the spirit of the particular Hour and should take into consideration the liturgical season or feast. They ought to draw the people together as a liturgical assembly and help them enter into the rhythm of the liturgy. Selections are given in the revised rite, but those who prepare the Liturgy of the Hours are free to choose hymns within the repertoire of the assembly.

The intercessions, Lord's Prayer and concluding prayer are dealt with next in the *Instruction* (#179 – 200). A distinction is made between the intercessions at morning prayer, which are properly invocations commending the day to God (#181), and the petitions at evening prayer, which are similar to those at Mass. Traditionally, the final petition at evening prayer is always for the dead (#186). The document reiterates that prayers of petition should always be linked with praise of God (#179, 185). Because they are also the prayer of the whole church, the petitions should be universal in character (#187). It is permissible to include particular intentions (#188), but the practice of inviting spontaneous intercessions often leads to the stating of purely private intentions. Both education and caution are needed in this area.

In the revised rite, the intercessions include a two-part petition and an invariable response. These can be prayed in different ways: The leader prays both parts of the petition and the assembly adds the invariable response, or the leader prays the first part of the petition and the assembly finishes with the second part (#189 – 193).

The *General Instruction* clearly lays out the ideal for the intercessions, but their actual forms in the revised rite are inconsistent in style, language and content. They are perhaps the weakest part of the whole revised rite. This is unfortunate, because intercessory prayer is one of the two main structural parts of the Liturgy of the Hours.

The Lord's Prayer (#194 – 196) follows the intercessions. When both morning and evening prayer are celebrated in addition to daily Mass, the age-old practice of praying the Lord's Prayer three times a day is sustained. Finally, the concluding prayer (#197 – 200) completes both Hours. It is taken from either the four-week cycle of the psalter or is proper to the festal seasons and feasts. It is the same as the opening prayer for Mass. It belongs to a priest or deacon, if one is present, to say this prayer in communal celebrations (#197). The *General Instruction* makes no comment about the closing blessing.

Chapter three concludes with comments on the importance of sacred silence (#201 – 203). The *General Instruction* suggests that an appropriate period of silence may be observed before the psalm prayer and after the scripture reading, either before or after the optional responsory (#202). Also, depending on how the intercessions are structured, there may be an appropriate time for a brief silence after the announcement of the petition (#193). It cannot be stressed enough that silence is an important part of liturgical prayer; its purpose is "to receive in our hearts the full sound of the voice of the Holy Spirit and to unite our personal prayer more closely with the word of God and the public voice of the church" (#202).

Chapter four

Chapter four focuses on special days and celebrations during the liturgical seasons: Sunday (#204 – 207), the Easter Triduum (#208 – 213), the Easter season (#214), the Christmas season (#215 – 216), solemnities and feasts of the Lord (#217) and commemorations of the saints (#218 – 224). It also details the arrangement of the Office for solemnities (#225 – 230), feasts (#231 – 233) and memorials (#234 – 240). The last part of the chapter discusses options for choosing an Office or particular texts (#241 – 252). These options lend variety to the Liturgy of the Hours but also are a source of confusion because people may have to turn to different parts of the book during a given prayer to find all the options.

Such special days and celebrations can be used fruitfully for parochial implementation of the Liturgy of the Hours. When a cathedral style of celebration is used in conjunction with a worship aid for the assembly, the prayer can flow smoothly and simply. It is important that the liturgy — especially in the choices of the hymn, intercessions, concluding prayer and blessing — reflect the spirit of the feast or occasion.

Chapter five

This final chapter concerns itself with the rubrics to be followed when the Liturgy of the Hours is celebrated in common. Several points are important for us here.

The function of the presider (or in the absence of a priest or deacon, the prayer leader) is to begin the introductory verse ("O God, come to my assistance"), introduce the Lord's Prayer and say the concluding prayer, blessing and dismissal (#256). Although the *General Instruction* does not mention it, the presider (or prayer leader) would also pray the psalm prayers.

The function of the cantor is to intone the antiphons, psalms and canticles (#260). The *General Instruction* indicates that either the priest or another minister may lead the intercessions (#257), but since they are properly sung, it would seem that the cantor is the more appropriate choice.

During the gospel canticles at morning and evening prayer, incense may be used (#261). The minister incenses the altar, the priest and the assembly. It also seems proper to incense both the paschal candle (if there is a *lucernarium*) and the book of the scriptures. It has become customary to use incense during Psalm 141 ("Let my prayer rise like incense") if it is one of the selected psalms for evening prayer. When incense is used during the singing of this psalm, it is a penitential gesture. We might bless or "wash" ourselves with the smoke in a penitential manner. When incense is used during the gospel canticles, it is a joyful sign of praise. An effective gesture is to lift up the incense as a sign of this praise. A simple liturgical dance also might be fitting at this time.

Standing is the appropriate posture during the introductory verse, hymn, gospel canticle, intercessions, Lord's Prayer, concluding prayer, blessing and dismissal (#263). The assembly is seated during the reading (unless a gospel text is proclaimed) and during the psalms and non-gospel canticles (#265). The usual form of the sign of the cross is made during the introductory verse (if it is used) and at the beginning of the gospel canticles (#266). When morning prayer begins with the invitatory, a sign of the cross is made on the lips.

Singing is a critical element in the Liturgy of the Hours, especially for the hymns, psalms, canticles and responsories, which are lyrical by nature (#269). If the intercessions are in litany form, they also might be sung. In #273, the principle of "progressive solemnity" is examined at some length. This principle recognizes various degrees of festivity with respect to celebrating the Liturgy of the

Hours and the important role music can play in varying the liturgy. For example, more of the liturgy might be sung on Sundays and feasts than on weekdays in Ordinary Time. Singing adds a festive element to the major seasons as well. Thus, music can help us better experience the rhythm of the liturgical year.

The *General Instruction of the Liturgy of the Hours* lays out many principles and guidelines, but a careful reading of the document and an examination of all the cross-references leads to the conclusion that the *Instruction* is intended to open the prayer to pastoral adaptation rather than restrict it. Many adaptations not only are permitted but are even suggested. At the heart of the *General Instruction* is the desire to adapt the prayer to the needs of the praying community. Of course, the *Instruction* seeks to ensure that the Liturgy of the Hours is celebrated carefully and with all the dignity that any liturgy deserves. There is also a clear desire that those celebrating the Liturgy of the Hours respect its tradition, especially its chief elements. Without psalmody and intercessory prayer, there is no Liturgy of the Hours. At the same time, however, the call to make the Liturgy of the Hours the daily prayer of all believers, not just the professionals, often requires that several adaptations be made. This is both an invitation and a challenge to parishes and other liturgical communities to enthusiastically embrace the Liturgy of the Hours, to make it the prayer through which they join the whole church in the unending song of praise and thanksgiving. Let us not waste this opportunity!

Strengths and Weaknesses of the Revised Rite

Fortunately, the revised rite retained some of its choral character. The antiphons, hymns and canticles invite singing; they are musical by nature. The variety of texts also is conducive to reflective prayer, which is helpful for both those who pray the Liturgy of the Hours daily and those who pray this prayer alone.

That same variety which is an asset to those who gather daily for this prayer can be a weakness on the parish level, where daily attendance at morning or evening prayer is less likely. The familiarity that is so important to good ritual prayer comes only after patient and regular exposure to the rhythm of the liturgy and its prayer texts. A beginner faced with the four-volume official rite and an *Ordo* is more likely to be overwhelmed by the choices than to be edified by the variety! The scripture readings and their responses nurture reflection and edification. Care needs to be taken, however, so that the contemplative element does not overshadow the liturgical character of the prayer, thus endangering the liturgical celebration of the paschal mystery as an expression of the ministry of the Christian assembly. The complexity of this prayer also can cause us to lose sight of its two central elements, psalmody and intercessory prayer.

At the beginning of this chapter we noted how Pope Paul VI, in his promulgation of the revised rite for the Liturgy of the Hours, emphasized that this prayer is the prayer of the *whole* church; it is no longer the exclusive prayer of clerics and religious. Nevertheless, while emphasizing the universal character of the Hours, *Laudis canticum* subtly assumes that the ordained remain the primary group toward whom the revision is directed. "[A]ccount was taken," it says, "of the circumstances in which priests engaged in apostolic works find themselves today" (#1). Thus there seems to be a built-in tension. Is the Liturgy of the Hours fundamentally the daily prayer of the whole church, or is it primarily the obligatory prayer of priests and deacons? There are different requirements for each.

The revised rite reflects this tension in its ritual structure. Because the Liturgy of the Hours is the prayer of the whole church, there is a marked emphasis in the revised rite on the two hinge Hours of morning and evening prayer. These two Hours clearly retain more of the characteristics of the ancient cathedral style, which facilitates parish celebration. The psalms, for example, are carefully chosen to fit the time of day and are sometimes repeated on a weekly basis (e.g., Psalm 51 on Fridays and Psalm 110 on Sunday evenings). The inclusion of antiphons (pointing to a responsorial style of cantoring the psalms) and psalm prayers aids the people's understanding. Generally, morning and evening prayer are more praise-oriented and exhibit a spirituality that directly relates them to our entry into the paschal mystery.

Many elements of the monastic style, however, were retained in order to make this prayer more attractive to people who normally pray the Hours alone. The use of almost the entire psalter over a four-week cycle, the inclusion of canticles from both Hebrew and Christian scripture and brief scripture readings may be an asset in contemplative prayer, but they are problematic on the parochial level. If a parish community were to take a rigid approach to the revised rite, frustration would be inevitable because the revised rite is not well-suited to parish liturgical needs. The conflicting needs of both groups result in a tension that remains one of the greatest weaknesses of the revised rite.

All is not lost, however. Often overlooked are the many ways that the revised Liturgy of the Hours can be celebrated by exercising its options. *Laudis canticum* made it clear that one of the goals of the revision was to adapt the rite "to suit the way of life and vocation of different groups dedicated to the liturgy of the hours" (#1). Surely one of those "different groups" is the local parish community. We might reasonably conclude that whatever the group, they have ample latitude for adaptation. Unquestionably, the prayer style of monastics differs from that of the pastor praying alone or of parishioners gathered in their parish church. This simple truth is too often forgotten.

Adaptation

At first glance, the Liturgy of the Hours is a confusing and complex prayer. Even monastic groups who are well trained in the art of praying the Liturgy of the Hours usually adapt the official rite to their own circumstances. Of all our liturgical rites, probably the Liturgy of the Hours has the strongest history of continual adaptation. There are a number of legitimate adaptations that better enable various groups to enter into the spirit of this prayer while capitalizing on the strengths of the official rite and minimizing its weaknesses. We will consider some of these in the next chapter.

While the need to adapt the Liturgy of the Hours to meet parish needs is acknowledged, these adaptations should not be determined by personal tastes, time constraints or any other shallow motivations. The revised rite offers a sound liturgical structure. Adaptations need to remain "legitimate," that is, authentic and faithful to the original. Basically, any adaptation that is made must respect the general structure of the rite, in which the psalms and intercessions are central.

No revised rite will ever be perfect. A casual look at the history and development of liturgy teaches us that adaptations are necessary in order to fit different times and cultures. It thus would be naive to expect the 1971 revision of the Liturgy of the Hours to completely satisfy our need for daily prayer. However, there is ample room to adapt this revision to suit the needs of different communities. The revised rite has some inherent difficulties, but that is no excuse to be lax in its parochial implementation.

While we await a further revision of the ritual, the challenge will be to take up the work of adaptation that will make the Liturgy of the Hours suitable to local needs so that real liturgical renewal can take place.

This renewal of the liturgical life of the church will not come to fruition simply by introducing more or different prayers. It will not come about merely by going through the motions of praying together. Real renewal occurs when our prayer is expressive of our privileged relationship with God through Christ. Renewal occurs when we experience our own participation in the paschal mystery. Renewal occurs when the Spirit leads us to an ever deeper understanding of ourselves as the body of Christ.

Chapter Four

A Closer Look:
The Structure and
Flow of the Rite

I t is one thing to evaluate the strengths and weaknesses of a rite, as was done in the last chapter, and quite another to live with those elements in a particular pastoral situation. To help familiarize planners with the ritual texts for morning and evening prayer, thereby providing a basis for considering appropriate adaptations, a closer look at the structure and elements of these rites is necessary.

Getting to Know the Rite

A good way to get to know a liturgical ritual is simply to read through the text. The official four-volume text of the *Liturgy of the Hours* might be too confusing for beginners. *Christian Prayer* is a one-volume edition of the official text. It contains the complete texts for morning, evening and night prayer, as well as selections from daytime prayer and the Office of Readings. *Shorter Christian Prayer*, as its name implies, is an abridged version of *Christian Prayer*. Either of these two books would provide an adequate starting point. Page through the ritual and note the general structure of morning or evening prayer and the various elements used in the rite.

Psalms

The psalms are distributed over a four-week cycle. Which psalms are most appropriate for morning prayer? for evening prayer? These questions might be best answered by praying particular psalms over a period of time. Note which ones best reflect the appropriate time of the day.

Intercessions

Notice the format and style of the intercessions for both morning and evening prayer. How are they alike, and how do they differ? How does the format for the intercessions compare with the format we normally use at Mass?

Propers

Notice that festive and seasonal celebrations are high-lighted by special texts called "propers." Propers are antiphons and prayers specifically appointed for that particular day or season. What are the advantages/disadvantages of this? What is most suitable for this parish/liturgical community?

Experience

It would be helpful for those who wish to introduce the Liturgy of the Hours on the parish level to gain some experience praying morning and evening prayer. Find out when morning and evening prayer are scheduled in neighboring parishes, in religious communities or in the diocese, and participate in those celebrations. A broad-based experience with this prayer on the part of those parish leaders who will implement it is crucial. What works in one parish or for one liturgical community may not necessarily work for another, but the exposure will be valuable.

Psalmody and intercessions form the backbone of both morning and evening prayer. Although the structures for both morning and evening prayer in the revised rite are quite similar, the characteristic emphasis underlying each prayer is different. In the following outline, the parenthetical elements invite adaptation.

Morning Prayer

Invitatory and Psalm 95
Hymn
Psalm (antiphon, *Gloria Patri* and psalm prayer)
Canticle (antiphon)
Psalm (antiphon, *Gloria Patri* and psalm prayer)

Reading (homily and responsory optional)
Gospel Canticle/Benedictus (antiphon)
Intercessions or Litany of Praise
Lord's Prayer
Concluding Prayer
Blessing
Dismissal

When morning prayer begins the day (the usual situation at the parish level), it opens with an "invitatory" consisting of an invitation to praise God ("Lord, open my lips"/"And my mouth will proclaim your praise") and Psalm 95 (Psalms 100, 67 or 24 may be substituted). The invitatory psalm captures well the spirituality of morning prayer: praise, worship and a readiness to live the day in God's presence. Dawn is a symbol of the resurrection, one of the dominant themes of morning prayer. The invitatory is followed by a variable hymn of praise that enables us to express our delight with the gift of a new day and our joy in dedicating it to God.

Psalmody and Word of God

Two morning psalms with their antiphons, *Gloria Patri* and psalm prayers (vestiges of a choral and community setting) are separated by a canticle from the Hebrew Scriptures that serves to remind us of events that are part of our salvation history. The psalmody is followed by a short reading and response. The reading is normally only a few lines long and is generally a passage not used in the *Lectionary for Mass*. The inclusion of scripture is reminiscent of the monastic *lectio continua*, but its brevity and non-sequential selection suggest that the primary purpose of morning prayer is less a reflection on the word of God than it is a pure prayer of praise.

Intercessions

Both the gospel canticle (Benedictus) and the intercessions underscore the strong element of praise in this prayer. The intercessions are properly either invocations directly addressed to Christ or a litany of praise. They dedicate the day to God and ask for help in living the day in a Christian manner. The Lord's Prayer and a collect prayer conclude the intercessions, and a blessing and dismissal complete morning prayer.

Evening Prayer

The structure of evening prayer is similar to that of morning prayer. The exceptions, however, help us understand the different character and emphasis of this prayer.

Introductory versicle and response
Gloria Patri
Hymn
Psalm (antiphon, *Gloria Patri* and psalm prayer)
Psalm (antiphon, *Gloria Patri* and psalm prayer)
Canticle (antiphon)
Reading (optional homily and responsory)
Gospel Canticle/Magnificat (with antiphon)
Intercessions
Lord's Prayer
Concluding Prayer
Blessing
Dismissal

An introductory verse ("God, come to my assistance"/"Lord, make haste to help me") and an evening hymn mark this prayer as appropriate to the waning day. A sense of our dependence upon God and a spirit of recollection and thanksgiving characterize the psalms chosen for this

Hour. A New Testament canticle follows the two evening psalms. It calls to mind the mystery of redemption, which reaches its climax in the life of Jesus. The intercessions are properly petitionary in form and primarily universal in content. The final petition at evening prayer is always for those who have died.

Although this structure is similar to that for morning prayer, the variations help us understand that evening prayer expresses sentiments proper to the end of a day: thanksgiving, sorrow for wrongdoing, rededication and recognition of our dependence on God. Notice that the *lucernarium*, an important part of cathedral prayer, is not found in the official rite and that neither is the sign of peace, which often concluded the cathedral Hours. Note also that in the rite there are no texts for Saturday evening prayer. Instead, Sunday evening prayer has two forms: Sunday Evening Prayer I, which is used on Saturday evening, and Sunday Evening Prayer II, which is prayed on Sunday evening.

Suggestions for Adaptation

Each praying community must prepare its celebration of the Liturgy of the Hours in a style that will suit its situation and needs. Obviously, the parish council celebrating evening prayer around the council table will pray differently than the community gathered at sundown on Easter Sunday to pray the evening prayer that concludes the Triduum. One strength of the revised Liturgy of the Hours is its adaptability; it is probably more fluid in its official structure than any other liturgical rite. Planning teams have a wonderful opportunity to shape the rite in a way that accords with the lifestyle(s) of the praying community and truly draws the assembly into a spirit of praise and petition.

Introductory rites

The use of the introductory versicle and response used at
evening prayer ("O God, come to my assistance"/"O Lord,
make haste to help me") and a similar versicle used at
morning prayer needs some consideration. In the earlier
structure of the Office, the hymn followed the psalmody.
Then the introductory verse served to open the Hour.
In the present structure, however, the hymn precedes the
psalmody and functions as an opening hymn, thus ren-
dering the introductory versicle and response redundant.
In more simple celebrations of the Office, it is perhaps
best omitted, especially if there is an entrance procession.

Psalmody

The psalmody of morning and evening prayer consists
of two psalms, each with antiphons, *Gloria Patri* and
psalm prayer, and a scripture canticle with its antiphon.
In most parochial situations, this is probably too complicated and lengthy to be effective prayer. If simplification
is necessary, perhaps the canticles could be omitted. It
would be preferable to retain the psalms, however, because
along with the intercessory prayer, they form the structural backbone of this liturgy. Ideally both psalms would
be retained, but at times it might be beneficial to pray
only one of them. Such might be the case when a community is just beginning to pray the Liturgy of the Hours
or when the assembly is primarily made up of children.

Antiphons

Because the antiphons assigned to each psalm properly
belong to responsorial singing, it is suggested that they
be used only when the community is able to sing the
psalms. The antiphons have long been seen as lending the
psalms a christological character. There is some disagree-
ment about whether the psalms can stand alone as prayer

in their own right or need to be interpreted as referring to Christ. But the Liturgy of the Hours is not a christological prayer because of added references to the second person of the Trinity; it is christological because this prayer of praise and intercession is our normative way of entering into the paschal mystery and because as a community of believers, Christ is always present with us as our high priest.

The *Gloria Patri* has traditionally concluded each psalm in the cathedral tradition. From a structural viewpoint, however, the gospel canticles (Benedictus and Magnificat) function doxologically, and hence the use of the *Gloria Patri* as part of the psalmody is redundant.

Scripture

The scripture readings assigned to morning and evening prayer also may present a problem. Often these readings are out of context and are so brief that they are not particularly meaningful for a parochial community. Furthermore, a community that also celebrates daily Mass would hear four scripture readings proclaimed in one day (i.e., two at Mass and one each at morning and evening prayer). That could be too much to grasp. The *General Instruction of the Liturgy of the Hours* (#46) permits the use of another passage which may be taken from the Office of Readings or from the day's Mass texts.

It might be helpful if the readings assigned to a particular day's Mass were integrated into morning and evening prayer. For example, in place of the designated reading for evening prayer, the text assigned as the first reading from the *Lectionary for Mass* for the following day would be proclaimed at evening prayer. The gospel of the day from the *Lectionary for Mass* would then be proclaimed at morning prayer. (The tradition of excluding gospel texts at morning and evening prayer is not followed in this case.) This kind of approach draws the community into the readings from the *Lectionary for Mass* and gives people time to reflect on the readings and live them before they are proclaimed during the eucharistic liturgy of the word. In some communities, fewer words can be better. For others, however, the richness and variety of readings is essential and so the proclamation of four different scripture readings each day is a pastorally effective option.

Progressive solemnity

The liturgical calendar provides us with a natural impetus for varying the degree of solemnity in the Liturgy of the Hours. Weekdays, especially during Ordinary Time, call for simple celebrations. More festive would be feast days and Sundays, and the most festive celebrations would be solemnities and festal seasons. A parish or liturgical community might use a simpler style of prayer with smaller groups (e.g., to open or close parish meetings) and a more festive style when the Liturgy of the Hours is celebrated with the whole parish (e.g., on Sunday evenings). School children also might benefit from a simpler style of prayer. The simplicity or complexity of style is determined by structural components, the amount of singing and movement, the number and role of ministers and the use of light and incense.

A basic, simple celebration might include an opening hymn, the recitation of one or two psalms, sufficient time for reflection after each psalm (lending a more contemplative flavor to the prayer), a scripture reading followed by another moment of silent prayer, sung intercessions, and the blessing and dismissal. Even if only one psalm and a very short reading were used, the length of this prayer would seem appropriate for daily communal prayer before or after work or at a parish meeting.

A more festive celebration might add vested ministers (alb and stole in the case of a priest), sung psalmody, the *lucernarium* (light service) if it is evening, and the use of incense during Psalm 141 as well as during the gospel canticles. Processions, a brief homily and the use of additional musical instruments and liturgical vesture (e.g., a cope) could further add to the air of festivity.

The possibilities for adapting the Liturgy of the Hours are many. Good ritual prayer, however, calls for consistency and repetition so that parishioners can move beyond the mechanics of the prayer to an authentic spirit of praise and thanksgiving. We need to become so accustomed to this pattern of prayer that it becomes a part of us, so much so that whenever we are unable to pray morning or evening prayer, we truly do miss it. Our awareness of that void gently calls us back to faithfulness to the prayer. The enthusiasm engendered by those who experience the richness of this prayer will move the beginnings toward fulfillment.

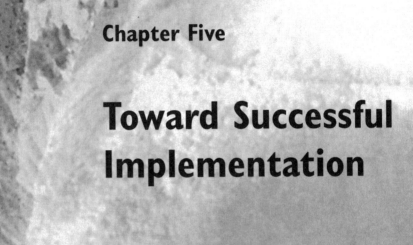

Chapter Five

Toward Successful Implementation

The most formidable challenge to implementing morning and evening prayer in a parochial setting is not becoming convinced of the need and advantages of praying this liturgy on a daily basis. The most formidable challenge is addressing the questions of how to convince others of the need and value of this type of prayer and how to proceed so that a positive response is elicited. While there are no sure-fire answers to these questions, a carefully prepared agenda enhances the chances for success.

Initial Steps

At some point, the implementation team simply must take the plunge and schedule a celebration of morning or evening prayer. Even this first attempt, however, should flow from prior reflection and increased pastoral sensitivity. Let common sense be the guide. The following suggestions might aid the planning team in their task.

1. Become familiar with the rite

It is paramount that those charged with initiating the Liturgy of the Hours be themselves very familiar with the rite. The material in chapter four provided a way to begin that process. This familiarity needs to be of two kinds: First, planners must be familiar with morning and evening prayer as a ritual that they themselves have prayed, preferably in more than one style. It is awkward to implement a ritual with which we are not completely familiar and at ease. This leads to the second kind of familiarity: The planning team also needs to understand the theology, structure and stylistic options inherent in the rite in order to make the best possible choices for their particular community.

In both academic and pastoral work, a simple principle holds: You have to know the rules before you can break them! If we begin with a solid theological foundation, then the specific choices we make will flow from that theology and be consistent with it. This ensures that liturgy preparation is not short-circuited by the preferences or whims of any individual or committee. Further, it ensures that we have a solid grasp of the whole ritual and a sense of how the parts fit together. Our tendency is to skip this part of the preparation and not articulate the theology from which we work.

Questions and considerations that might help an individual or committee articulate a theology of the Liturgy of the Hours include:

- How does this daily prayer reflect the paschal mystery?

- Which elements of the prayer are essential, and which are secondary?

- On what occasions is a more simple prayer appropriate? When is a more festive style of prayer called for? What elements give the prayer a more festive character?

- What is the relationship between the Liturgy of the Hours and both weekday and Sunday Eucharist?

- What is the relationship between the liturgical seasons and morning and evening prayer?

- How is the structure of the Liturgy of the Hours essentially a dialogue between God and the community of believers?

- In what way are the psalms the prayer of contemporary Christians?

- How is the communal character of this prayer evident?

- What is the relationship of music to liturgical prayer?

2. Develop a long-range plan

Don't be discouraged if initially you are not successful!
Parochial prayer practices will not change overnight. This
is especially true with respect to daily Mass and devotions.
Simply replacing daily Mass with morning or evening
prayer is bound to cause problems.

A long-range plan begins with an evaluation of the overall
schedule of community prayer in the parish. This evaluation includes taking a critical look at the Sunday and daily
Mass schedules. The liturgical renewal of Vatican II has
increased our appreciation for eucharist. Often, however,
the eucharistic liturgy has become the only way in which
the community gathers to pray. A long-range plan also
needs to examine the devotional prayer practices of the
parish. Some parishes schedule special devotions only
during Advent and Lent. It is unfortunate that such practices rarely get carried over into the actual festal times
for which Advent and Lent prepare us.

The idea behind a critical evaluation is not to create a vac-
uum but to work toward a balance between liturgical and
devotional prayer. This balance also includes different
styles of prayer so that the needs of various subgroups in
the parish can be addressed. Too often, we take for granted
that our schedule of liturgical prayer and devotions meets
the needs of all the members of the parish or liturgical
community. We also must recognize that, as communities
change, what is helpful and satisfying to one group may
not be so helpful to the evolving community.

3. Inform and educate

Once while I was teaching a class on the Liturgy of the
Hours, the students asked that we schedule a time to pray
morning prayer together. This experience revealed a
two-fold challenge: On the one hand, it is difficult to talk

about — let alone get people to be enthusiastic about — a prayer with which they have had absolutely no experience. But on the other hand, although people are motivated by good experiences, a positive experience without sufficient background to reflect on it rarely leads to long-term change. Successful implementation of the Liturgy of the Hours includes a serious educational element.

Education does not (and probably should not!) mean a series of lectures on the subject. We tend to follow an academic model for the continuing education of adults, but this way of going about it has not been rousingly successful in most cases. How can planners inform and educate the community about this prayer before, during and after it has been introduced and implemented?

One good way to begin is with short, repeated bulletin inserts that incrementally lead the community toward an understanding of the Liturgy of the Hours. Several samples follow:

- Many of us grew up praying simple prayers when we awoke in the morning and before we went to bed at night. The morning offering or the Angel of God prayer are good examples. The church, too, has a traditional morning and evening prayer called the Liturgy of the Hours.

- The Liturgy of the Hours is part of the church's official public prayer that we call "liturgy." As such, it is best celebrated in a communal setting. We join our voices with the voice of Jesus in offering an unending hymn of praise to God.

- The Liturgy of the Hours is the church's daily pattern of prayer. It is based on the natural rhythms of sunrise and sunset. In the morning, we offer praise and thanks for the gift of a new day. In the evening, we seek forgiveness for our failings, offer God thanks for the wonder of the day and beg for God's continuing mercy. Thus our days and our lives are framed in prayer.

- The basic structure of morning and evening prayer consists of psalms and intercessions. The psalms express our deepest human emotions and place them in God's hands. Through the prayers of intercession, we confidently present to God our own needs and the needs of the whole world.

- A more familiar title for Liturgy of the Hours might be "Divine Office." Recent history understood this prayer to be the concern of priests and religious. Now the church wishes to restore the Liturgy of the Hours to its original function as the daily prayer of all those who are baptized.

- The Liturgy of the Hours offers us a fuller experience of the church's rich treasury of prayer. This prayer both prepares us for a more fruitful celebration of the eucharist and sustains in us its benefits throughout the day.

Once these short "information bytes" have generated some comment and curiosity, a somewhat more extensive sharing of information might take place. This may take the form of lengthier bulletin inserts that provide simple explanations of the theology, development and structure of the Liturgy of the Hours. Andrew Ciferni, OPRAEM, has prepared an excellent four-part series of bulletin inserts on the Liturgy of the Hours. Reprint information is available from the Federation of Diocesan Liturgical Commissions in Washington, D.C. At some point during this sharing of information, a simple morning or evening prayer should be scheduled. The next three steps help in this regard.

4. Begin modestly

A great disruption or massive change in the prayer life of a parish guarantees alienation and failure. After the critical evaluation (Step 2 above), share the results as well as your plans for the future with the parish. Decide on a tentative schedule for morning and/or evening prayer for the next year. A careful and gradual introduction is most effective. Be wary of replacing or dropping practices, especially if they are long-standing patterns. The objective is to expose parish/liturgical community prayer to a fuller expression of the paschal mystery, not to condemn or alienate people. Introduce what you know will be well received. Focus on groups that may feel ignored. Bear in mind that this will be a long-term commitment.

5. Start with small groups

Greater success in implementing the Liturgy of the Hours is more likely when some members of the parish understand the Liturgy of the Hours and are sufficiently familiar with its structure to celebrate it well and with ease. The parish staff and liturgy committee might pray morning or evening prayer whenever they gather at those times for meetings. Some parish staffs begin each day of ministry with morning prayer together. Parish council members, because of their leadership role in the parish, would benefit from exposure to this prayer. Children and teachers in the parish school or religious education program should experience this prayer on a regular basis. Candidates for initiation could be as leaven in the parish while they learn the value of this tradition. Those who serve as liturgical ministers in the parish might be encouraged to pray morning or evening prayer as part of their continuing spiritual formation. The Liturgy of the Hours is also an excellent format for ecumenical prayer services. Confirmation retreats for teens could include morning or evening prayer. Even the *Order of Christian Funerals* encourages the use of morning and/or evening prayer. Special texts are included specifically for this purpose (*Order of Christian Funerals*, Part IV). Talk freely with parishioners about this experience of liturgical prayer.

As this prayer becomes familiar to more and more parishioners, their own delight and commitment to it will be infectious. Other parish groups — scripture study groups, prayer groups, base communities, families — could be encouraged to begin praying the Liturgy of the Hours. Someone in the parish should be available to guide their choices. Though there is ample room in the revised rite for adaptation to local needs, too much freedom with the structure may destroy its *liturgical* character. The prayer's connection to the paschal mystery must be respected. In other words, the Liturgy of the Hours is not meant to be devotional prayer.

6. Move from simple celebrations to more festive ones

Initial celebrations with small groups ought to be simple but not lose the character of liturgical prayer. A simple introductory rite that serves to transform those gathered into a liturgical assembly, psalmody, intercession and a concluding blessing are sufficient for an authentic experience of the Liturgy of the Hours. In any setting, the two key elements of psalmody and intercession are always the focal point of this prayer. Music is normative in any liturgical celebration. Thus the hymns, acclamations, greetings and antiphons should be sung whenever possible. Singing better emphasizes the sense of praise that is so basic to morning and evening prayer, and this is especially true of the psalms.

A fuller cathedral style of prayer can be scheduled for the parish or liturgical community after the basics are in place. Make sure the ministers are well-rehearsed so that newcomers to this prayer can feel at ease. Again, do not allow a less-than-full church to be discouraging. If it is a good celebration, gradually the numbers may increase. Repetition and a sense of reverence are hallmarks of long-term success.

7. Schedule special, then weekly, then daily celebrations

Major holidays are probably not the best times at which to introduce the Liturgy of the Hours. On Christmas and Easter parishioners will be busy with family events, although that is not true for everyone. The celebration of Evening Prayer on Easter Sunday is particularly encouraged despite potential conflicts, because as the concluding liturgy of the Triduum, it is a wonderful opportunity to once more experience the mystery and awe that have permeated the preceding three days.

The seasons of Advent and Lent are usually good times for initiating morning and evening prayer on a regular basis, but we must avoid creating the impression that the Liturgy of the Hours is "penance." Special parish occasions, times of diocesan celebrations and the feasts of saints meaningful to the parish (especially the patron saint of the parish) are better times to introduce the Liturgy of the Hours. Set a precedent, and then schedule the celebration again for the following year.

From occasional celebrations a parish can move toward regular weekly celebrations on Saturday or Sunday evenings. This pattern acknowledges the importance of Sunday and provides the liturgical assembly with another opportunity to gather. Once weekly celebration has been established, daily celebration is the next step. At this point it is good to recall that these celebrations of the Liturgy of the Hours do not all have the same degree of festivity. Weekday liturgy is always less festive than Sunday liturgy.

8. First evening prayer, then morning prayer

The average parishioner is more likely to be available in the evening than in the morning. Combining evening prayer with other evening events (e.g., parish meetings or educational programs) is a good way to familiarize people with this liturgy and to emphasize that this prayer is the daily prayer of the church, not a passing fad.

Once a regular pattern of evening prayer has been established, morning prayer can be introduced. At this point it is good to remind ourselves that the objective is not to get *everyone* there but to gather a *representative* assembly. Given most people's busy schedules, it is unrealistic to expect the majority of parishioners to attend morning or evening prayer on a regular basis. Nevertheless, when the body gathers, the *whole* body is present. Encourage parishioners to choose for themselves the day or season that best suits their coming to morning or evening prayer, and then encourage them to be faithful to that time. This way, there will be more than a small handful present and a habit will be established. The key is to make sure that this is liturgical prayer. If people experience a sense of God's presence, they will return. When preparations and celebrations become ho-hum and ritualistic, efforts will falter no matter how well-intentioned they are.

Preparing and Celebrating

After a celebration of evening or morning prayer has been scheduled, the immediate preparations begin. A liturgy preparation team works out the details of the liturgy, ministers are assigned, the environment is carefully tended and rehearsals are scheduled. Careful attention to these details is critical to the quality of any liturgy.

Preparation

In the beginning, it is helpful to repeat the same prayer patterns for a while so that people become familiar with the ritual style and its music. Gradually, the musical repertoire of the parish can be expanded. Elements of the prayer should be chosen not only for their individual appropriateness but so that the liturgy is a coherent whole.

Worship aids can help the assembly familiarize themselves with the rite more quickly. If the planning team prepares these aids, they should be handsomely presented. Be sure to secure any necessary copyright permissions. With larger groups and on festive occasions, emphasize the cathedral elements of the prayer.

Ministers and ministries

By definition, liturgical prayer involves people in differing roles — Liturgy of the Hours is no exception. The need for various ministers is an important consideration. Musical accompanist(s), choir, acolytes, greeters and dancers all enhance the celebration. More festive occasions call for more ministers. At the very least, an assembly, presider and cantor are essential. Let us briefly look at the various ministers and their roles.

The assembly has as its first ministry to manifest the church, the people of God, the body of Christ. Secondly, in surrendering to the liturgical action, the assembly enters into the death/resurrection mystery of Christ and continues the ongoing work of redemption. Furthermore, just as in all liturgical celebrations, the assembly is the most important music minister at the Liturgy of the Hours. Other music ministers never sing *for* the assembly; those ministers have their own proper role. To pray and sing as one is a wonderful sign of the unity of the body. The hymn, antiphons and responses properly belong to the music ministry of the assembly.

The presider (or prayer leader) does more than recite special texts. The ministry of the presider, whether ordained or lay, is to monitor and facilitate the prayer of the entire assembly. Several key factors aid this ministry. First, the presider must *pray*. This is not as easy as it sounds. Because the presider is responsible for the overall unfolding of the celebration, he or she will naturally be concerned with what comes next or what adjustments must be made spontaneously to catch the "mood" of the assembly during a particular celebration. The presider must be completely familiar with the structure and flow of the prayer, both in general as well as in specific celebrations.

Furthermore, it is the presider who determines the flow and pace of the celebration. The presider must "read" the silences and know when the assembly is ready to move on. Even a very short period of silence can seem like an eternity to someone who is nervous. To help new presiders or prayer leaders judge the length of the silence, they might silently count to a certain number or say a Hail Mary or the Lord's Prayer. As presiders become more adept at "reading" the silence, these artificial ways of keeping pace gradually will be eliminated. In a sense, the presider's attention is always divided. On the one hand, he or she is focused *inward* as a praying member of the assembly; on the other hand, he or she is necessarily focused *outward* as the one monitoring the progress and quality of the assembly's prayer. Finally, the presider must be comfortable enough with the prayers, ritual gestures and actions (such as placing incense in the censer) so that they can be done with grace, beauty and ease. It is often helpful to rehearse these movements.

The cantor has an indispensable role in the Liturgy of the Hours. The ministry of the cantor is to facilitate the assembly's prayer of praise and petition. Ideally the cantor leads the intercessions during a simple weekday liturgy and sings the verses of the psalms if the assembly is not able to. The cantor also may lead the assembly in singing the hymn and responses.

The reader proclaims the scripture passage and does so from within his or her lived experience of that word. In the context of liturgy, reading requires more than public speaking skills. True proclamation includes conveying to the assembly that there is hope and promise in God's word, that the word challenges, that the word is to be lived. The ministry of the reader is to allow God's word to come alive in the lives of the assembly. To do this, the reader obviously must be familiar with the scripture passage. The scripture passage needs to be studied and rehearsed *before* arriving at the celebration site. The ability to speak distinctly and to project one's voice so that the reading can be easily understood are the starting points for successful ministry.

Acolytes or assistants may be needed for more solemn or festive celebrations of the Liturgy of the Hours. The acolyte processes in with the presider and cantor and assists the presider with the book and censer. The assistant might incense the altar, presider and assembly during the gospel canticle. The ministry of the acolyte is one of quiet and unobtrusive service. It is an important ministry because it adds festivity to the celebration and allows the presider to gesture freely and be more present to the assembly. On such festive occasions, the acolyte might vest in an alb.

An accompanist(s) may or may not be present at a simple daily celebration but is essential for a festive celebration. This ministry supports the assembly's sung prayer. A prelude and postlude would enhance the celebration on Sundays and on solemnities. The musician might accompany the cantor during the psalm, although it might be better not to accompany the cantor during the intercessions so that the cantor has more freedom to pace the intercessions according to the prayer needs of the assembly.

The choir can bring much festivity to a solemn celebration. They can add harmony to the hymns, psalms and responses and might do a meditative response to the reading. Like the ministry of the cantor, the role of the choir is an important one but should never replace the music ministry of the assembly itself. Inviting the choir to sing is also an excellent way to expose them to this form of prayer.

Greeters or hospitality ministers may be present on very festive occasions. Just as on Sunday, their ministry is to greet those gathering in the name of God and to welcome them in such a way that their transformation into an assembly gathered in the name of the Lord will be facilitated.

Dancers or a liturgical gesture group can add much solemnity to a festive celebration of morning or evening prayer. Two moments in particular lend themselves to graceful, beautiful movement. Dancers carrying lighted candles might accompany the paschal candle in the entrance procession of an evening prayer service beginning with the *lucernarium*. This is especially powerful when the sacred space is clothed in darkness and the dancers move among the assembly to dispel the darkness and surround them in the light of Christ. Liturgical movement also can be effective when combined with the incensation during Psalm 141 or the gospel canticle. Care must be taken that this ministry, like all liturgical ministries, is carried out with reverence and solemnity. Ministry is never entertainment but is meant to draw the assembly deeper into the liturgical action.

Environment

Various items that might be needed to celebrate morning or evening prayer include a Bible or lectionary, a presider's chair, an ambo or lectern, musical instrument(s), incense, the paschal candle, a processional cross and liturgical vesture. The more festive the celebration, the more these elements might be used. Make choices carefully and purposefully. Be careful that the service is not so overloaded with symbols that those assembled lose sight of what is essential. The basic principle for all liturgical environment is that it should draw attention to what is central. In the case of the Liturgy of the Hours, the ambo, presider's chair and paschal candle (if used) are the focus.

The space should be arranged to facilitate the movement
of the prayer. If the psalms are prayed antiphonally, it
is best for the chairs to be arranged in two facing sections.
(This may be impossible with pews.) If the Liturgy of
the Hours is celebrated in a church, the altar is not emphasized because it is not a focal point in this ritual.

Rehearsal

Until ministers become very familiar with the rite, it is
helpful to rehearse the ritual with them. It may work
best to have the ministers gather an hour before the scheduled time of prayer. This usually allows for sufficient
rehearsal time and ensures that the procedure is fresh in
the ministers' minds. In general, the more elaborate the
celebration, the more time needed for practice. A specially
prepared "presider's edition" of the liturgy, containing
the complete order, text and music for the liturgy, can be
of great assistance to the leader of prayer.

Even after ministers know the ritual, most will occasionally
need to be reminded of basic liturgical principles. Pacing
is often one of the biggest problems. We tend to pray
too fast, especially if we are reciting the psalms on a daily
basis. We need to frequently remind ourselves that a
measured pacing of our psalms lends a musical quality to
the prayer. When that rhythm is disrupted or is too fast,
the prayer can become "sing-songy" or even distracting.

Underlying Challenges

There are two things that regularly seem to cause some
difficulty in implementing the Liturgy of the Hours in
a parochial setting: our practice of "once-a-week religion"
and daily Mass. Further reflection shows, however, that
these are not insurmountable obstacles.

Once-a-week religion

Unlike many of our non–Roman Catholic sisters and brothers, many Roman Catholics have grown up with the unfortunate misunderstanding that "church" means Mass on Sunday. Although Sunday is the day *par excellence* for the gathering of believers, it hardly relegates the other days of the week to a mundane and profane realm. Special devotions and meal prayers are frequently a part of people's religious tradition, but often there is little, if any, connection between these daily practices and the Sunday assembly.

Our baptismal commitment challenges us to think of Christian living in a holistic sense in which the days give meaning to each other and open up onto the richness of Sunday. The paschal mystery sanctifies all of time and puts to rest the dualism between "earthly" life and "heavenly" life. There is a "connectedness" that keeps us in constant relationship with the paschal mystery. Our private prayer practices are important then because they keep God's gracious presence before us and help us recognize God's overtures of love. Private devotions are a means for enriching liturgical prayer and are a necessary part of our religious expression. Even if we pray morning and evening prayer on a regular basis, we still must maintain some kind of personal prayer life. This does not necessarily refer to formal prayers such as the rosary or novenas, but it does mean that in all of the ups and downs of our everyday living, we often turn our minds and hearts toward God. Slowly, as this discipline begins to shape us, God is revealed as the center of our lives and not just a Sunday visitor.

Daily Mass

Often we assume that more of a good thing is better. Though we certainly do not want to diminish the worth of this preeminent celebration of the resurrection, we also dare not conclude that it is the *only* liturgical celebration. In fact, daily celebration of the Mass runs the risk of turning Mass into a devotional practice which can obviate the weekly rhythm of the paschal mystery, a rhythm that prepares us in its own special way for the Sunday celebration.

If the celebration of the eucharist is reserved primarily for Sundays (funeral liturgies, for example, would be an exception), and if we respect nature's daily rhythm of dying and rising, then the need for a prayer such as the Liturgy of the Hours becomes clear. Both historically and theologically, *the Liturgy of the Hours is the proper daily celebration of the paschal mystery.* When Christians gather, especially at the critical morning and evening hours, it is natural that they pray together.

Even if a parish or liturgical community does not yet celebrate morning and evening prayer on a regular basis, parish liturgy committees need to discuss the relationship between daily Mass and the Liturgy of the Hours. The *General Instruction of the Liturgy of the Hours* does allow for the possibility of combining one of the Hours with Mass (#93).

This option is helpful for liturgical communities that have a regular habit of celebrating morning and evening prayer in addition to Mass each day. However, be aware that the style for praying the Hours is necessarily different from the style for celebrating the eucharist.

Should eucharist and the Liturgy of the Hours be combined? There is no definitive answer to this question because pastoral situations differ. The best solution would be to weigh the pros and cons and choose a course of action that balances respect for the rituals with the reality of daily life.

Epilogue

Saint Paul exhorts us in his letter to the Thessalonians:

"Rejoice always, pray without ceasing,
give thanks in all circumstances;
for this is the will of God in Christ Jesus for you.
(1 Thessalonians 5:16 – 18)

The daily rhythm of sunrise and sunset has for centuries provided Christians with a natural cycle for gathering for prayer. The Liturgy of the Hours developed as a formal expression of the need to set each day in the context of praise and petition.

The particular format of this prayer was dependent on the needs of the community. In cathedral parishes, the Liturgy of the Hours was closely connected to the time of day at which it was prayed; it was highly structured and repetitive. In monastic communities, where the community was stable and prayer was frequent, there was a greater need for variety. In both settings, however, the psalms and intercessions were central elements of the prayer.

Gradually over the centuries, the Liturgy of the Hours moved away from its original role as the daily prayer of all the baptized. By the middle of the twentieth century, it was popularly understood as the specialized prayer of priests and religious. The Second Vatican Council called for a restoration of this prayer so that it could again truly be liturgy — the work of the people. Though this renewal is underway, much work remains to be done.

Many people today are seeking a genuine and deep relationship with God. Sunday Mass, of course, remains the primary source of interaction between God and God's people, but people continue to look to the church and its ministers for other ways to daily express their profound desire to praise and thank God and to beg for God's favor. The Liturgy of the Hours responds to these needs. Those who hunger for a deeper dimension to their lives are a valuable asset for implementing the Liturgy of the Hours in our parishes and other liturgical communities. Well-prepared and reverent celebrations of morning and evening prayer invite us to a closer union with the death and resurrection of Jesus.

We will know we are successful when our prayer allows us to surrender ourselves to a loving God who transforms us ever more perfectly into the body of Christ here on earth. We will know we are successful when our prayer becomes an ongoing dialogue with God, whose words continue to echo in our lives. We will know we are successful when, one with Christ and his church, we raise an unceasing chorus of praise, singing an ever new song unto God's glory and honor.

Glossary

Antiphon   A short refrain, usually a paraphrase of a line from the psalms or other scriptures, that is repeated by the assembly during the singing or recitation of a psalm or canticle. Its purpose is to highlight a particular interpretation of the psalm or to better express the liturgical season.

Benedictus   Latin title for the Canticle of Zechariah (Luke 1:68 – 79). This song of praise and thanksgiving is the usual gospel canticle at morning prayer.

Breviary   Common name for the book used before the reforms of Vatican II containing the Liturgy of the Hours. It was intended for private use. The breviary was an abridged form of the monastic Office, which required the use of several different books at each Office. Its name is derived from the Latin word for "short."

Canticle   A hymn or song of praise and thanksgiving usually taken from the scriptures but not from the psalter. The major canticles are taken from gospel texts: the Canticle of Zechariah (Benedictus), the Canticle of Mary (Magnificat) and the Canticle of Simeon (Nunc Dimittis). These are the gospel canticles prayed at morning prayer, evening prayer and night prayer, respectively. Other canticles from both the Hebrew and the Christian scriptures are also used at morning and evening prayer.

Compline   Night Prayer. The final prayer of the day in the Liturgy of the Hours. It is prayed at bedtime.

Constitution on the Sacred Liturgy   The first official decree of the Second Vatican Council, promulgated on December 4, 1963. Also known by its Latin title, *Sacrosanctum concilium*, this document put forth broad principles for liturgical reform, including the celebration of the liturgy in the vernacular, increased participation by the assembly and the reform of the liturgical year and the Liturgy of the Hours.

Cursus   The cycle of assigned psalms in the Liturgy of the Hours.

Daytime Prayer   Any one of the Hours of Terce, Sext or None in the Liturgy of the Hours. Normally only one of these three Hours is prayed on a given day.

Divine Office   The name often used to refer to the Liturgy of the Hours before the reforms of Vatican II. Also known simply as "The Office."

Gloria Patri   Latin name for the brief prayer of praise to the Trinity which concludes each psalm in the Liturgy of the Hours. "Glory to the Father, and to the Son, and to the Holy Spirit . . ."

Hour   One of the specific rites contained in the Liturgy of the Hours and usually related to a particular time of day. The 1971 revision recognizes seven Hours: Morning Prayer (Lauds), Evening Prayer (Vespers), Night Prayer (Compline), the Office of Readings (Matins or Vigils), midmorning prayer (Terce), midday prayer (Sext) and midafternoon prayer (None).

Invitatory   The short acclamation ("Lord, open my lips"/ "And my mouth will proclaim your praise") combined with Psalm 95 (or one of its substitutes) used to begin the Liturgy of the Hours each day.

Lauds   The Latin name for Morning Prayer.

Lectio continua   Latin expression referring to the tradition of reading the Scriptures in a sequential manner. The reading for each day begins at the point where the previous day's reading ended. This is the basic pattern used in the Office of Readings.

Lucernarium   (From the Latin *lucerna,* lamp) A service of light sometimes used to begin evening prayer although not officially a part of that liturgy.

Magnificat   Latin title for the Canticle of Mary (Luke 1:46 – 55), used each day at evening prayer.

Middle Hour   Any one of the Hours of Terce, Sext or None in the Liturgy of the Hours. Normally only one of these three Hours is prayed on a given day.

None   Midafternoon prayer in the Liturgy of the Hours. One of the three daytime prayers.

Nunc Dimittis   Latin title for the Canticle of Simeon (Luke 2:29 – 32), used each day at night prayer.

Office of Readings   One of the seven Hours in the Liturgy of the Hours. Normally composed primarily of three psalms and two readings (only one of which is from the Scriptures), the Office of Readings is not connected with a particular time of day; it can be prayed at any time.

Ordo   Name of the annual calendar that specifies the days on which feasts will occur. It also specifies the texts to be used at Mass and for the Liturgy of the Hours.

Proper   The prayer or hymn texts in the Liturgy of the Hours that vary according to the particular feast or liturgical season being celebrated.

Responsory   A short, optional acclamation following the scripture reading at morning and evening prayer, designed to enable the word of God "to penetrate more deeply into the mind and heart" of the listener or reader.

Sext   Midday prayer in the Liturgy of the Hours. One of the three daytime prayers.

Terce   Midmorning prayer in the Liturgy of the Hours. One of the three daytime prayers.

Vespers   The Latin name for evening prayer.

Resources

Official Texts

The Liturgy of the Hours. New York: Catholic Book Publishing Company, 1975. The official, four-volume edition of the complete Office for the entire liturgical year.

Christian Prayer: The Liturgy of the Hours. New York: Catholic Book Publishing Company, 1976. This official, one-volume edition of the Liturgy of the Hours includes Morning Prayer, Evening Prayer, Night Prayer and selections from Daytime Prayer and the Office of Readings for the entire liturgical year.

Sunday Celebrations in the Absence of a Priest. New York: Catholic Book Publishing Company, 1994. This book, prepared by the Committee on the Liturgy of the National Conference of Catholic Bishops, includes a ritual for morning and evening prayer (with optional Holy Communion) for use on Sundays in the absence of a priest. Both English and Spanish translations are included.

Order of Christian Funerals. Chicago: Liturgy Training Publications, 1989. The revised funeral rite suggests that "the vigil for the deceased may be celebrated in the form of some part of the office for the dead." Settings for morning and evening prayer, as well as a selection of hymns, are included in Part IV of the rite.

Sunday Celebration of the Word and Hours. Canadian Conference of Catholic Bishops, 1995. The official Canadian text for use by a layperson or deacon who leads the prayer at the Sunday gathering of a community when a priest is unable to be present. An order of service for both morning and evening prayer is given. The Pastoral notes offer valuable background information.

Documentation

"General Instruction of the Liturgy of the Hours." In *Documents on the Liturgy, 1963 – 1979.* Collegeville: The Liturgical Press, 1982. The official instruction that explains the manner in which the Liturgy of the Hours should be understood and prayed. The complete text can also be found in volume one of the four-volume edition of the Liturgy of the Hours.

"Laudis Canticum." In *Documents on the Liturgy, 1963 – 1979.* Collegeville: The Liturgical Press, 1982. The apostolic constitution of Pope Paul VI, dated November 1, 1970, which promulgated the revised edition of the Liturgy of the Hours.

Roguet, A.-M. *The Liturgy of the Hours: The General Instruction with Commentary.* Collegeville: The Liturgical Press, 1971. Along with the complete Instruction on the Liturgy of the Hours, Roguet's insightful commentary considers the theology, liturgy and spirituality of the Liturgy of the Hours.

Study Text VII: The Liturgy of the Hours. Washington, DC: United States Catholic Conference, 1981. This commentary serves as a practical aid for understanding and implementing the Liturgy of the Hours.

General Resources

Benvenga, Nancy, ed. *The Liturgy of the Hours: Your Guide to Praying at Home and in Your Parish Community.* Mineola, NY: The Resurrection Press, 1990. A practical overview that includes a basic introduction to the psalms and a helpful bibliography.

Brook, John. *The School of Prayer.* Collegeville: The Liturgical Press, 1992. Subtitled "An Introduction to the Divine Office for All Christians," this book offers basic principles for praying the Hours as well as a commentary on the official texts.

Bugnini, Annibale. *The Reform of the Liturgy, 1948–1975.* Collegeville: The Liturgical Press, 1990. An insider's view of the work of revising the Divine Office.

Campbell, Stanislaus. *From Breviary to Liturgy of the Hours.* Collegeville: The Liturgical Press, 1995. A detailed look at the structural reform of the Office, which took place between 1964 and 1971.

Campbell, Stanislaus. "Liturgy of the Hours." In *The New Dictionary of Sacramental Worship.* Collegeville: The Liturgical Press, 1990. An overview of the history and theology of the Divine Office.

Ciferni, Andrew. *The Liturgy of the Hours.* Washington, DC: Federation of Diocesan Liturgical Commissions, 1992. This four-part series of bulletin inserts would serve as an excellent introduction to morning and evening prayer in the parish.

Duggan, Robert. "Liturgy Checklist: The Church's Daily Prayer." *Church,* Spring 1989. New York: National Pastoral Life Center. A practical resource for groups seeking to implement the Liturgy of the Hours on the parish level.

Funk, Virgil. *Weddings, Funerals, Liturgy of the Hours.* Washington, DC: The Pastoral Press, 1990. Three of the essays in this collection, including one by Michael Joncas, offer reflections on the relationship of the Hours to the time of day and to time in general.

Gallen, John. *Christians at Prayer.* Notre Dame, IN: University of Notre Dame Press, 1977. Essays by William Storey and Frederick McManus examine issues related to the Liturgy of the Hours. (This book is out of print.)

Henderson, J. Frank. "Praise God Morning and Evening." *National Bulletin on the Liturgy,* **September 1988.** Ottawa: Canadian Conference of Catholic Bishops. Both the theory and practice of morning and evening prayer in the parish receive attention in this issue.

Irwin, Kevin W. *A Guide to the Eucharist and Hours.* Collegeville: The Liturgical Press, 1985 – 1991. This three-volume set (Lent, Advent/Christmas, Easter) provides a commentary on the texts of the Liturgy of the Hours for both the Sundays and weekdays of the seasons.

Jones, Cheslyn, et al., ed. "The Divine Office." In *The Study of Liturgy.* New York: Oxford University Press, 1978. A detailed look at the history of the Divine Office with a strong ecumenical perspective.

Larson-Miller, Lizette. "Introducing the Liturgy of the Hours," in *Modern Liturgy* **(March and April 1989).** San Jose, CA: Resource Publications. This two-part article provides both background information and practical suggestions for implementing morning and evening prayer in the parish.

Martimort, A. G. "The Liturgy of the Hours." *The Church at Prayer.* **Vol. 4.** Collegeville: The Liturgical Press, 1986. An in-depth examination of the history, theology and structure of this prayer.

McManus, Frederick, ed. "A Call to Prayer: The Liturgy of the Hours." In *Thirty Years of Liturgical Renewal.* Washington, DC: United States Catholic Conference, 1987. McManus offers an excellent commentary on the 1977 statement of the U.S. bishops promoting parish implementation of the Liturgy of the Hours.

Proclaim Praise: Daily Prayer for Parish and Home. Chicago: Liturgy Training Publications, 1995. A simple order of prayer for morning and evening. Includes some midday and night prayers.

Scotto, Dominic. *Liturgy of the Hours.* Petersham, MA: St. Bede's Publications, 1987. Includes both the historical background for the reform of the Hours and practical guidelines for implementation.

Zimmerman, Joyce Ann, ed. *Liturgical Ministry* 2, **Summer 1993.** Collegeville: The Liturgical Press. Includes "The Psalms in the

Liturgy of the Hours," by Carroll Stuhlmueller, "Theology, Styles and Structures of the Liturgy of the Hours," by Austin H. Fleming, and "Liturgy of the Hours: Pastoral Perspective," by Gerald T. Chinchar.

Resources for Celebrating Daily Prayer with Children

Huck, Gabe. *Hymnal for Catholic Students: Leader's Manual.* Chicago: Liturgy Training Publications, 1989. Chapter six of this manual, along with its accompanying hymnal, set the foundation for daily prayer with children.

Jeep, Elizabeth. *Children's Daily Prayer.* Chicago: Liturgy Training Publications, annual. Designed to be used by students in a classroom setting with a strong emphasis on liturgical feasts and seasons.

Vos, Joan Patano. *Celebrating School Liturgies with Children.* Collegeville: The Liturgical Press, 1991. Chapter three provides a format for morning and evening prayer with young students.

Musical Resources for the Liturgy of the Hours

I. G.I.A. Publications, Inc.

Gather, **2d ed.** 1994. Contains a setting each for Morning Praise and Evensong. More cathedral in style.

Gather Comprehensive. 1994. Includes same setting for morning and evening prayer as found in *Gather,* 2d ed.

Hymnal for the Hours. 1989. A collection of 316 hymns to be used in conjunction with the Office book.

Light and Peace. David Haas. A complete musical setting of morning and evening prayer for use in parishes and other liturgical communities.

Praise God in Song. Ecumenical Daily Prayer. John Melloh and William Storey, eds., 1979. Contains three complete settings of morning and evening prayer by Howard Hughes, Michael Joncas and David Isele.

Worship, **3d ed.** 1986. Settings for morning, evening and night prayer. Leader's edition also available. More monastic in style.

II. The Liturgical Press

The Collegeville Hymnal. 1990. Offers 23 hymns and canticles for Morning and Evening Prayer.

Pray Without Ceasing: Prayer for Morning and Evening.
Zimmerman, et al., 1993. Original settings for morning and
evening prayer for liturgical seasons, solemnities and feasts.

III. Oregon Catholic Press

O Joyful Light.   Michael Joncas. Complete settings for morning
and evening prayer.

Journeysongs.   1994. Basic settings for morning and evening prayer.

IV. World Library Publications

God of Light Be Praised: Music for Evening Prayer.   1995. Seasonal
settings from a variety of composers, commissoned for the twenty-
fifth anniversary of the Notre Dame Center for Pastoral Liturgy.

People's Mass Book.   1984. Contains basic settings for morning and
evening prayer.

We Celebrate.   1994. Volume one of this three-volume program
contains simple settings for morning, evening and night prayer.

V. Liturgy Training Publications

*Morning and Evening: Order of Service for Presider, Cantor and
Accompanist.*   Joyce Ann Zimmerman and Kathleen Harmon, 1996.
This leader's edition contains the texts and music for seven evening
and three morning prayer services. The introductory notes provide
a helpful guide for beginners. To be used in conjunction with *Morning and Evening,* an aid for the assembly, also published by LTP.

Morning and Evening.   Joyce Ann Zimmerman and Kathleen
Harmon, 1996. A participant's aid for celebrating morning
and evening prayer in the parish. Ten settings cover the entire
liturgical cycle. To be used in conjunction with *Morning and
Evening, An Order of Service for Presider, Cantor and Accompanist.*

Psalms for Morning and Evening Prayer.   1995. Contains the psalms
and canticles used in morning and evening prayer based on the
ICEL translation. Includes music and pointed psalm texts .

VI. *Lutheran Book of Worship.*   Minneapolis: Augsburg Publishing
House, 1978. Contains settings for morning, evening and night
prayer.

VII. *The Hymnal 1982.*   New York: The Church Pension Fund,
1985. Contains 46 hymn settings for morning, evening and night
prayer in the Episcopal Church. To be used in conjunction with *The
Book of Common Prayer* by the same publisher.

Publishers

Augsburg Fortress Publishers
Box 1209
426 S. Fifth Street
Minneapolis, MN 55440
Tel: 800-328-4648
Fax: 612-330-3455

Canadian Conference of Catholic Bishops
Publications Service
90 Parent Avenue
Ottawa, Ontario
K1N 7B1
Tel: 613-241-9461

Catholic Book Publishing Company
77 West End Road
Totowa, NJ 07512
Tel: 201-890-2400
Fax: 201-890-2410

Church Pension Fund
800 Second Avenue
New York, NY 10017

Federation of Diocesan Liturgical Commissions
401 Michigan Avenue, NE
PO Box 29039
Washington, DC 20017
Tel: 202-635-6990

G.I.A. Publications
7404 South Mason Avenue
Chicago, IL 60638
Tel: 800-442-1358

The Liturgical Press

P.O. Box 7500
St. John's Abbey
Collegeville, MN 56321
Tel: 800-858-5450
Fax: 800-445-5899

Liturgy Training Publications

1800 North Hermitage Avenue
Chicago, IL 60622-1101
Tel: 800-933-1800
Fax: 800-933-7094

National Pastoral Life Center

299 Elizabeth Street
New York, NY 10012-2806
Tel: 212-431-7825
Fax: 212-274-9786

Oregon Catholic Press

5336 NE Hassalo
Portland, OR 97213
Tel: 800-548-8749
Fax: 503-282-3486

Oxford University Press

198 Madison Avenue
New York, NY 10016
Tel: 800-451-7556
Fax: 212-726-6455

The Pastoral Press

5640-D Sunnyside Avenue
Beltsville, MD 20705
Tel: 301-474-2226
Fax: 301-513-5924

Resource Publications

160 E. Virginia Street
Suite 290
San Jose, CA 95112-5876
Tel: 408-286-8505
Fax: 408-287-8748

The Resurrection Press
Box 248
Williston Park, NY 11596
Tel: 800-892-6657
Fax: 516-746-6872

St. Bede's Publications
Box 545
Petersham, MA 01366-0545
Tel: 508-724-3407
Fax: 508-724-3574

World Library Publications
A division of J.S. Paluch Company, Inc.
3825 N. Willow Road
Schiller Park, IL 60176
Tel: 800-621-5197
Fax: 708-678-2911

United States Catholic Conference
3211 Fourth Street, NE
Washington, DC 20017-1194
Tel: 202-541-3000

University of Notre Dame Press
Notre Dame, IN 46556
Tel: 800-621-2736